13 FATAL ERRORS MANAGERS MAKE*

*AND HOW YOU CAN AVOID THEM

13 FATAL ERRORS MANAGERS MAKE*

*AND HOW YOU CAN AVOID THEM

W. STEVEN BROWN

Fleming H. Revell Company
Old Tappan, New Jersey

Scripture quotations in this volume are from the King James Version of the Bible.

Quotations from MARY KAY ON PEOPLE MANAGEMENT © 1984 by Mary Kay Cosmetics, Inc. Published by Warner Books.

Excerpts from *Seeds of Greatness* by Denis Waitley copyright © 1983 by Denis E. Waitley, Inc. Published by Fleming H. Revell Company. Used by permission.

Excerpts from *The Double Win* by Denis Waitley Copyright © 1985 by Denis E. Waitley, Inc. Published by Fleming H. Revell Company. Used by permission.

Library of Congress Cataloging in Publication Data

Brown, W. Steven.
   13 fatal errors managers make.

   On t.p. an asterick is following "make" in the title.
   "*And how you can avoid them."
   1. Supervision of employees.   2. Personnel management.
I. Title.   II. Title: Thirteen fatal errors managers make.
HF5549.B865   1985   658   85-8245
ISBN 0-8007-1423-7

To the members of the Fortune Team—
those who are on the job each day and
to our family members and loved ones
who have given so unselfishly of themselves and
encouraged us in our efforts to
"help others help themselves."

ACKNOWLEDGMENTS

This book would not have been possible without the efforts of many people. I'm especially thankful to the thousands of managers who have been willing to share their experiences—both good and bad—with me. I will be forever grateful to Charles Josey for his collaboration and efforts in helping me translate my thoughts and spoken words into a readable format.

CONTENTS

Preface   9

FATAL ERROR #1:
Refuse to Accept Personal Accountability   17

FATAL ERROR #2:
Fail to Develop People   29

FATAL ERROR #3:
Try to Control Results Instead of Influencing Thinking   41

FATAL ERROR #4:
Join the Wrong Crowd   54

FATAL ERROR #5:
Manage Everyone the Same Way   62

FATAL ERROR #6:
Forget the Importance of Profit   74

FATAL ERROR #7:
Concentrate on Problems Rather Than Objectives   81

FATAL ERROR #8:
Be a Buddy, Not a Boss   89

FATAL ERROR #9:
Fail to Set Standards   99

FATAL ERROR #10:
Fail to Train Your People   108

FATAL ERROR #11:
Condone Incompetence   126

FATAL ERROR #12:
Recognize Only Top Performers   137

FATAL ERROR #13:
Try to Manipulate People   146

PREFACE

For fifteen years the Fortune Group and I have been helping businesses succeed and managers manage. In that time I've seen just about every kind of business situation. And after all these years in the trenches, solving real, not textbook, problems, I have discovered that companies fail primarily because managers fail. And when managers fail it is not because they cannot master numbers, but because they try to master people, or manipulate them, or ignore them.

In a recent *Megatrender* newsletter, John Naisbitt put the issue this way:

> Industry's challenge: shifting from managers who traditionally (and supposedly) had all the answers and told everyone what to do, to managers who act as facilitators, as developers of human potential. *For the re-invented, information-age corporation of 1985 and beyond, the challenge is retraining managers, not retraining workers.*

As demanding a bottom-line manager as Harold Geneen, who built ITT from a sleepy little company to one of the great conglomerates, agrees with this point of view. In his book *Managing,* he says this about the art of management: "Leadership is the very heart and soul of business management. No one really manages a business by shuffling the numbers or rearranging organizational charts or tallying the latest

business school formulas. What you manage in business is people. . . .
To my mind, the quality of leadership is the single most important in-
gredient in the recipe of business success."

What's This Book About?

It's about perfecting your leadership and managerial skills by avoiding the common errors managers make with the people they manage.
I'm giving you the truly classic mistakes. Indeed, managers have been
making the same ones since Abel tried to supervise Cain. And they can
prove fatal—if not for you, for your company. But you don't have to
perpetuate any of these common defects of managerial character,
habit, style, and judgment, if you know what they are. And, luckily for
you, there are not many: I recognize just 13! In the hundreds of companies that the Fortune Group has served in the United States, Canada, and Australia, we have scrupulously cataloged all the most
common managerial errors that occur in business situations that
have gone sour. The words to describe the situations may differ, but the
underlying problems seldom do. This book shows you these 13 all-too-
common traps, so that you will never again fall into them.

Why So Negative, Steve?

When I shared my idea for this book with friends and business acquaintances, I naturally got a lot of free advice. I always listen and look
when something's free. After all, if I can't convince the people I know
and who like me, how am I going to convince you? The most common
criticism I got was not about the insights and information, but about
the approach. "Why look at the negative?" people asked. One friend
advised me to call it *13 New Ways for Winners to Win*.
    "Take a look at the best-seller list," some of my positive-thinking
friends advised me. "Business books focus on success." But I contend
that too many books give you beautiful examples you can't use. You
may feel impressed, even awed, by X Corporation's brilliant gambits,
but you end up frustrated. It's not always inspiring to read about the
excellence of others when your own managerial affairs seem to rival
those of Job. The impact of too many of these positive books becomes
negative, because you wind up feeling deficient.
    I'm not saying you can't learn from a good example: My Sunday-
school teacher believed it, and so do I. But haven't you noticed that
good examples seem to change with the times, while bad examples remain perennial? As I'm writing this introduction, for instance, the issue
of *Fortune* magazine on the stands analyzes what went wrong, in the
1984 economic slowdown, with some of the companies Peters and Waterman had portrayed as paragons of management in their book *In*

Search of Excellence. That does not mean that they were wrong in
their choices, but only that situations change—and so do fortunes, if
you make Fatal Errors.

Ask yourself: "What was my best learning experience and greatest
triumph as a manager?" What story do you tell the boys (or the girls) in
the office when it's show-and-brag time? Don't you describe that time
you pulled the fat out of the fire, busted out of some complex bottle-
neck, overcame some difficulty, climbed out of some hole, or got a brilliant insight after getting a black eye? If you're like me, you learned
about cars by working on clunkers. You felt good about your successes,
but you learned more from your failures. Every good manager I've ever
met says the same thing. In fact, I believe that the real distinctive of
American know-how lies in the Yankee attitude of tackling problems
head-on and hands on.

Learning what went right for others may not always give you much
insight about what's going wrong for you. However, I've seen the same
things wrong for a thousand different managers, watched them make
the same 13 Fatal Errors, and I know for an absolute certainty: *You
can learn from their mistakes!*

Because their mistakes are probably your mistakes.

"Well, okay," you say. "I can learn from negative examples, but why
the hype and high drama, Steve? Trying to sell a few extra books with
'Fatal Errors'?" Sure! It makes for a juicier title. But let me tell you a
little story, so you'll get my drift.

My personal computer has a troublesome little prompt line in the
word-processing package that comes up more often than I like. When I
get things all bollixed up, it flashes the message FATAL ERROR on the
bottom of the screen. So, more than a few times, I've had occasion to
hunt through the manual to get the meaning of that "error message."
The definition is short and to the point (rare for that incomprehensible
manual). It says: "The file you are trying to format or print is somehow
messed up because you've given contradictory commands." Most management errors are of the same sort. Someone sent out contradictory
signals, and the process got fatally messed up.

The true art of management, I believe, lies not in the art of winning,
as popular business books so often characterize it; rather it demands
the art of winning assent. It is the art of clearly communicating and di-
ligently monitoring tasks and goals, then fairly rewarding the people
who achieve them, because they have made a commitment to them on
the basis of corporate good and personal interest.

Who's the Book For?

This book is for managers or anyone who wants to be one someday.
Old managers. Young people just starting their business careers.

And especially for women as increasing numbers enter the managerial ranks.

Old managers need this book because they've been doing some things wrong so long, they think they're right. If they have reasonably successful careers or have reached a certain level of authority, probably everybody tells them that they are right about everything. And that's wrong. Fatally wrong.

Young people need this book because the business world they see is nothing like the one they read about—not in business school and not in novels. They know something is going on, but it's like watching a Balinese dance. You know all those hand, foot, and eye movements mean something. But what? Every young manager has read all about motivating employees, but then they run into old Kurtz, who is forty years their senior and two ranks their junior, and he tells them it can't be done that way, it was never done that way, and it ain't going to be done that way.

It's even worse if Kurtz is one of your best producers.

Finally, I hope this book will prove especially useful to women. I spent a number of years successfully selling real estate early in my career, and the Fortune Group has worked with many sales organizations. Sales, the *New York Times* says, is the growth area for careers in the 1990s. I for one believe that sales will especially become a growth area for women. In real estate I saw the profession go from a white-shirt-and-tie business to a silk-blouse-and-tailored-suit profession. Because opportunities have expanded so greatly for women today, in sales and other areas of business, I want to correct a lot of baloney others have sold women about management. Some books try to frighten them by ominously asserting that management is a male ritual, based on military forms, competition, and the psychology of male bonding. They cite all the clichés about management terms based on sports talk: *go for it, take the ball, scoring, hit a homer.* These books like to scare women, because scare sells. They purport to give you "the inside stuff," and teach you "all the games mother never taught you" so women can compete in a man's world.

Think about it, though, in this light: Mike Vance, the nationally famous motivator and former Disney "imagineer," says that mothering is managing. No mother ever waited six months to give a performance appraisal to a kid who wants to dry the cat in the microwave. Mothers know how to manage conflict, correct and guide behavior, motivate subordinate peer groups, set goals for others, and get the garbage taken out, too. All this training is at least as significant as learning to hit the high inside ball and give the Cub Scout handshake. What mothers teach their daughters seems more applicable to today's management environment than what fathers teach their sons. As more women reach the highest echelons their style will become increasingly imprinted on business. Perhaps the change toward freer, more democratic organizations is as much an effect of women entering the work force as it is of higher education, to which we usually ascribe it.

Don't get me wrong. Though mothering may be management, management is not mothering. It requires, I firmly believe, the exercise of fine-tuning intuitions about people. Mark McCormack in *What They Don't Teach You at Harvard Business School,* describes it as people sense:

> Whether it is a matter of closing a deal or asking for a raise, of motivating a sales force of 5,000 or negotiating one to one, of buying a new company or turning around an old one, business situations almost always come down to people situations. And it is those executives with a finely tuned people sense, and an awareness of how to apply it, who invariably take the edge.

"Men are taught to talk, women to listen," my mother used to say. That's why I believe women have "the edge." Early they are taught to read others.

Mary Kay Ash, perhaps the most successful woman entrepreneur in American business puts it this way in her book *Mary Kay On People Management:* "Good managers are good listeners. God gave us two ears and only one mouth, so we should listen twice as much as we speak. When you listen, the benefit is two-fold: You receive necessary information, and you make the other person feel important."

Mark McCormack argues:

> The ability to listen, really to hear what someone is saying, has far greater business implications, of course, than simply gaining insight into people. In selling, for instance, there is probably no greater asset. But the bottom line is that almost any business situation will be handled differently, and with different results, by someone who is listening and someone who isn't.
>
> When I was preparing to write this book I asked a number of my business friends, several of them chairmen of companies, what business advice they would give if they were writing it. Almost without exception, and often at the top of their lists, they said, "Learn to be a good listener."

Management, I believe, is the art of winning assent to goals and of reaching them through others. I dedicate this book to the goal of showing you how to avoid the common errors managers make and how to use your own style, personality, and talents to move others to use theirs to reach your common goal.

Each chapter helps you do just that. At the end of each chapter I've provided a convenient personal action form that we use in our Fortune Group training sessions to help managers target their flaws and act to change them. Be sure to fill out each form with the errors you wish to correct and avoid and follow a specific plan for putting your insights to work on your job right away.

If I do no more than confirm for you that you do some things right and help you identify one thing that you do wrong, then this book will have succeeded in its goal of helping you become a more effective leader and more successful in your career.

13 FATAL ERRORS MANAGERS MAKE*

*AND HOW YOU CAN AVOID THEM

FATAL ERROR

1

Refuse to Accept Personal Accountability

First we must take a look at business success. What basic elements make it? And what is the real key to it?

The Five Prerequisites for Business Success

These five elements are essential to any organization's success:

1. A quality or unique product
2. Proper timing
3. Adequate capital
4. People resources
5. Effective management

But if you lack the fifth element, you will not have the first four. Why? Take a look at the influence the final one will have on the first four. Without effective management, correct decisions cannot be made about the product's features and the proper time for its introduction into the marketplace. The company lacking proper management cannot acquire, much less sustain adequate capital. Above all, it takes good management to attract the best people and to coach and develop them. Every forward-looking manager recognizes that the greatest untapped resource within any company is its people's potential. As managers, we have the responsibility to unleash this vast store of talent.

17

One chief executive of a major American firm said: "Take my assets—but leave me my organization, and in five years I'll have it all back." Success in business never comes as a happy accident; it is built through the efforts of honest, responsive-reactive management and maintained the same way. You might say that management is the key to success.

If You Don't Stop the Buck, It Stops You

In business, everything begins and ends with management. And in order to work effectively, management must be accountable. When Harry Truman was president of the United States, he had a sign in the Oval Office: THE BUCK STOPS HERE. Each manager should adopt the same dictum. If you look at your organization and don't like the people, don't blame them; the fault lies with you. If you don't like your volume of business, look at yourself, not just at the market. If you don't like your percentage of profit, don't blame inflation; take a hard look at how you are operating. The buck must stop with management. And if you don't stop it, ultimately it stops you. The effective manager accepts personal responsibility for results.

When management finds itself in trouble and the danger signals begin to flash, we often hear managers say, "Well *my* office is different—*my* territory is different."

Baloney! No office or territory is "different." When a manager makes such a statement, he may kid himself, but he doesn't kid anyone else. He actually means, "Hey, don't evaluate me by the same criteria you use to evaluate other people. Don't judge me on the same basis you judge others; if you do, I'm going to fail. But as long as you'll go along with the idea that my territory is different, the territory fails, and my hands remain clean."

Choose Your Path

Essentially there are two actions in life: *performance* and *excuses*. Make a decision as to which you will accept from yourself—and those you manage.

Two distinct and entirely different attitudinal approaches exist, based on these actions, and only one manages successfully. Internalists, those who are performance oriented, accept personal accountability for their actions, successes, and failures. They know that if they feel unhappy with their results, they have only to look into a mirror to stare the culprit straight in the eye.

Others refuse to accept their responsibility for their position in life and hide behind excuses. Because they constantly blame some external source, condition, or other people for their personal failures, we'll call them externalists. We'd rather not call them managers.

The Failure Formula

We may predict and calculate the amount of failure an individual will experience by this formula: *People fail in direct proportion to their willingness to accept socially acceptable excuses for failure.* Externalists abound, and their socially acceptable excuses form a list that would fill volumes. An abridged list includes such statements as: "I'd be successful, if it weren't for my teenage daughter." "Let me tell you, I'd be making it, if it weren't for the interest rate." "I'd really be on top of the world today, if it weren't for the Internal Revenue Service." "You know, I'd really be successful, if it weren't for the Federal Reserve Board." "We would really be making it in my branch, if it weren't for the policies that come down from corporate management." "You know, we would really be successful, if it weren't for this, that, or the other." Listen closely to an externalist, and you'll hear him position himself as a victim. Being a victim, in his view, gives him a claim on the sympathy of others. It means he's not responsible for what happens, and therefore he escapes the responsibility for his own failure.

The internalist, on the other hand, takes the hand life deals him and plays it to the best of his ability. When I think of internalists, my mind always goes to a close personal friend of mine, Walter Frank, who is one of the most successful Realtors® in Canada. Until Walter was twenty-seven years of age, he was a successful cattle farmer. During his twenty-seventh year, he awoke one morning to find himself paralyzed with polio and realized that he would lose the use of his legs for the rest of his life and would be in a wheelchair. An externalist, in Walter's situation, would have given up. He had a powerful excuse not to be a successful farmer. But internalist Walter Frank did not give up. With his previous profession no longer possible, he looked around to see what else he might do. A friend suggested he might try sales. Walter chose the field of real estate, even though it presented many hardships. He found it practically impossible to get into many of the homes, but he would have his prospects go into the recesses that were unavailable to him; then he would talk with them about their reactions, both good and bad. He found that in a wheelchair, he could go door to door and talk to people about listing their property. In his second year in the business, Walter became the number-one salesperson in all of Oshawa. After three years in real estate, he opened his own company and today operates one of the most successful real-estate companies in all of Canada. A story of courage, a story of determination? Really, it's a story of a man willing to accept personal accountability for his life rather than a socially acceptable excuse for failure. In management, we just cannot escape the fact that we must be internalists. To manage effectively, we must have the ability to lead others, and people will follow only those whom they respect. Respect is earned by accepting personal accountability. Now, this *doesn't* mean we will succeed in every endeavor or that we'll reach every objective and always come out on top. But it *does* mean that if we experience failure, if things do not go our way, we can say, "Hey, I failed. It was my fault. Here's what I learned. I'll not make the same mistake again, and I can turn this failure into a future success."

The Three Unspoken Words

An important facet of accountability is being able to admit you are not all-knowing. Weak managers never say these three words: "I don't know." Instead they respond, "Let me get back to you on that," and waste half a day trying to ferret out the answer in order to save face. Others opt for condescension and say, "I think the information will be more meaningful to you if you dig it out for yourself." Still others simply lie and hope that their best guesses are correct.

All this seems especially foolish when we consider that the total knowledge of the human race now more than doubles each decade. (I cannot resist adding that I checked two sources for this time figure. Both experts made flat statements about the time it took to double man's knowledge. The two sources were adamant, but not in agreement. Neither would admit they weren't sure.)

When we dodge issues or duck the facts, when we pretend to know more than we do, we demonstrate a lack of emotional maturity, something that any leader greatly needs. Harold Geneen scores this point:

> One of the essential attributes of a good leader is enough self-confidence to be able to admit his own mistakes and know that they won't ruin him. The true test is to be able to recognize what is wrong as early as possible and then to set about rectifying the situation. I made my share of mistakes at ITT and they did not ruin me. I admitted them at general managers' meetings, often with the expression, "I guess I pushed the wrong button," and then I outlined my plan to save as much as could be saved from the situation. Usually such *mea culpas* were well received. Anyone who has made a goof gets a little enjoyment out of seeing The Man up there admit to one. There's nothing lost and much to be gained by admitting that you're human.

Each of us projects an image to the public, but we also have another image, a real one, that we admit privately (we call it our concept of self). The closer the public image we project is to our concept of self, the greater our emotional maturity.

The manager who lacks emotional maturity, who feels compelled to project the image of being all-knowing, of being the answer person, soon loses credibility and, consequently, destroys his ability to lead.

The manager who, in response to a question for which he doesn't have the answer, says, "You've posed an important question, and we need to know the answer; see if you can get it from one of these specific sources" sends an employee back to work with guidance, encouragement, and a compliment in the bargain. Such a manager has shown his emotional maturity and receives respect.

"They Made a Mistake"

The most unforgettable example of not accepting accountability I have ever encountered involves a segment from the television documentary series *60 Minutes.* The subject was crime and its effect on the victim and the perpetrator.

A robbery took place in a New York subway. During its course, the victim was shot. While the bullet didn't kill the man, he suffered a tremendous amount of brain damage and became practically a vegetable. Not only did the program document the effect on the injured man, it also showed the effect on his family. A chain reaction had been triggered: Since the man could no longer function, he lost his job; therefore mortgage payments couldn't be made, and the family home was lost. To make matters even worse, his wife had no marketable skills, so she had to work at menial tasks and try to hold the family together on social assistance. Heartbreakingly, this senseless crime spilled over from the victim to other innocents: his wife and children.

The second half of the coverage took place in prison, where a reporter interviewed the young man who had perpetrated the crime. When asked his opinion of his punishment, he responded, "Hey, man, they made a mistake! I'm not like these people, and they've got me locked up in here with criminals. I'm not a criminal! My crime was different. The only reason I shot the guy was he resisted when I tried to rob him!"

That young man remains totally out of touch with reality. And if released from prison, he will continue to shoot people, until he accepts personal accountability for his actions. I suggest that any time we, as managers, say, "My territory or my office is different," we become just as out of touch with reality. Only when we take personal accountability for our actions and their results can we truly begin to manage effectively.

A Philosophy of Management

I believe that one of the first steps in managing effectively is to evolve a definite philosophy of management. And we cannot have one until we can define *management*. In our years of experience in working with managers in all businesses, we at the Fortune Group have developed a definition of management that we believe expresses a very viable philosophy: "Management is the skill of attaining predetermined objectives with and through the voluntary cooperation and effort of other people." We believe the definition works because of the semantics—the words that make up the definition itself. Let me call three key words to your attention.

SKILL. Management is a skill because we may learn management techniques and, through practice, perfect them. You have an opportunity and obligation to become more adept at managing people. Because as a manager you "play" with the lives of other people, you should dedicate yourself to acquiring the knowledge necessary to liberate people to do their best work, to achieve and succeed.

ATTAINING. Management requires attaining. I didn't say management is the skill of working hard. It doesn't mean giving us your best effort or giving it the old college try. Management must focus on results.

At training sessions and seminars the Fortune Group conducts, I hear managers trying to outdo one another with stories of how hard they work. You would think that the big event of the day included the awarding of a folio of blue-chip stocks to the person with the most incredible story. But no prize gets handed out, because hard work merits none. Only results call for rewards. I know an excellent manager who tells those under her supervision, "Don't tell me about the labor pains; show me the baby."

In business management, professional sports analogies are frequently used. Study any sports story used to illustrate a point, and you will find the same fundamental point: You win or you lose; only in Little League do they honor effort for its own sake.

On one of my trips to work with the Royal Trust Company of Canada (a firm with over 6,000 salespeople), I asked a question of Lawrie Kingsland, who for many years served as director of training for this outstanding organization, "With all the managers you've had the responsibility of developing, can you tell me the difference between the really effective sales manager and the poor one?"

I've never heard anyone give a more succinct answer. He replied, "Steve, quite simply, the effective manager is the one who gets the job done."

That is all that really matters. We get no premiums in management for coming to the office at seven in the morning and staying until seven at night. No one gives out awards for not being able to play golf on Wednesday afternoons or for not spending a weekend with your family. Not getting a good night's sleep because one of your people calls you at midnight with a problem doesn't make you special. Don't expect premiums for any of this!

Management is a lot like golf. It's not *how*—it's *how many*. Recently, I played golf with friends. I had a hole-in-one! I hit the worst golf shot of my life. I skulled; I practically shanked a 7-iron. The ball went out to the right and hit a tree, bounced off, and came back to the fairway; then it hit a rock, rolled up on the green, and went straight into the cup. On the scorecard, I wrote, *1!*

When we won, my partner and I only talked about that ace, not my flubs, because it made no difference how I hit that ball; it was a 1—and that's all that counts. I've seen some of the "sloppiest" negotiating make the sale and the least textbooklike management achieve results. Remember that management is *not* the art of *doing* it like the pros—it's a skill of *achieving* like the pros.

One of my best friends is Dick Caruso, currently senior vice-president of Coldwell Banker/Residential Brokerage Services Division. Previously, Dick was president of RichPort REALTORS®, a Chicago-based organization that had twenty-seven different branches and about five hundred salespeople. I worked extensively with Dick and his company as a consultant. One night as we wrapped up our work and got ready to break for dinner, I asked Dick if I could help him with anything else while I was in town.

He thought a moment and said, "Yes, I would like to have you talk with one of our managers. It seems our business is not his vocation. Our business is his avocation; his vocation is cards."

I pressed for details and he said, "He shows up at his office and spends about an hour-and-a-half in the morning before going across the street to the country club where he plays cards all day long. Then he returns to the office and spends about an hour before going home."

"Dick, before I talk with him, tell me about his office. For starters, among your twenty-seven branches, where is his?"

"Oh, it's the largest."

"What about volume of business?"

"His office does more than any other branch."

"What about bottom-line profit?"

"Oh, it's our most profitable."

I thought we might have a case of a person spending a lifetime building a branch and deciding to semiretire himself at full salary, so I added, "Well, what about growth?"

Dick said, "Percentagewise, it grows more than any of the others. There's hardly any turnover among his salespeople, and they absolutely love him." Then Dick sighed, "Steve, what do you think we ought to do?"

I said, "I think we ought to find twenty-seven more just like him. He's the best executive in the bunch!"

Let's face it: That man did what all of us would like to learn to do. He found a way of managing that allows people to work to their fullest and to thereby increase productivity and profitability. Honestly, I couldn't do it, but just because *I* cannot doesn't mean that *he* can't. How long or hard any of us work means little; how much each of us produces, how much each of us attains from those under our supervision, is what really counts.

VOLUNTARY.　Management is based on attaining predetermined objectives with and through the *voluntary* cooperation and effort of other people. I think sometimes those of us in management forget that a business is not a shrine at which people worship, that a business, yours or mine, is simply nothing more than a vehicle designed to meet human needs and solve human problems. We meet human needs and solve human problems through our products and services. If we manage our business successfully and if we want to get the voluntary cooperation and effort of our employees, our business must meet the needs of those employees. I think far too many managers fall into the trap of believing that their employees are there to serve them, rather than to fulfill their own needs.

Several years ago I consulted with a sales organization in the state of Ohio, which had over four hundred salespeople, working primarily on a commission basis. One of the managers of the firm took me back to my hotel after the management session we had conducted that day, and he said, "Steve, I sure would like to have you talk with one of the saleswomen in my office."

I asked, "What about?"

He told me, "Well, she refuses to reach her potential. She could earn a minimum of one hundred thousand dollars a year; she's never earned less than fifty thousand dollars, but for the past two years she's refused to make more than thirty thousand."

Now to me that looked like quite an interesting situation, and I thought I might like to talk to her because it was so unusual, but I said, "Before I talk with her, tell me a little about her."

"What do you mean?"

"Well, why is she with you?"

"You know, she never wanted to work."

"What do you mean by that?"

"She was a teenage bride, got married in high school, never graduated. When she was twenty-six, her husband died and left no insurance. With two little girls and no marketable skills, she really took the only job she could get, selling water softeners door-to-door. She did this quite successfully, saved some money, capitalized herself, and joined us in our business. From the time she came to us, she's always been one of our top producers—never made less than fifty thousand dollars a year. Now her kids have grown and married, and she only wants to earn thirty thousand dollars. What do you think I ought to do with her?"

I told him, "I think you ought to go back to the office, hug her neck, get down on your hands and knees, and pray for four hundred just like her." Who says she has a potential of $100,000 a year? Her manager? Who says she should earn $50,000 a year? Her manager? Look at the woman's background: widowed, two little kids, got out in the snow, sold water softeners door-to-door, capitalized herself, came into his business, earned $50,000 a year. Now her kids are grown and married; she wants to earn $30,000 and spend the rest of the year traveling and visiting her grandchildren. Why not? That fills her needs.

I don't know why he thinks she ought to earn $50,000 or $100,000 but I've got a pretty good idea. You see, the more she earns, the more he makes. But I suggest to you that he could find five other people who would earn $50,000 a year and increase his own income much faster than he will ever force that woman whose needs are $30,000 to earn $50,000. If he keeps putting the screws to her, if he keeps pressuring her, he's going to lose her! And he should lose her! Because she's not there to serve him. She's there to meet to her own needs. Now, if she had had a territory tied up or her income had been below the company's minimum standard, that would have been a different story. But in that particular business no one had exclusive territories, and she sold well above the company's minimum standard. He cannot get her voluntary cooperation to do anything unless she's meeting her own needs as well as those of the organization.

The Leadership Barrier

What I'm about to say you may not like to hear. But if I don't mention it, I won't be honest with you. There is a fact of life that you must accept. If you hold a management position, every person you manage distrusts you. We all doubt management. We learned this from the teachings of Samuel Gompers and Jimmy Hoffa and George Meaney and I. W. Abel, among others. Incidentally, much of that teachings has a proper foundation. Candidly and honestly, historically management has been guilty of some pretty wicked abuses in dealing with people. If not, we would never have had our problems with child labor and sweatshops. Consequently, everyone has been taught and conditioned to some extent to believe that management will use you, that management will regard you as nothing more than a tool or a pawn to be used by management to reach management's objectives.

Because you care, you come up with an idea you evaluated on only one basis: Is it good for my employees? Will it offer them greater opportunity? Will it give them a greater chance for success? In your heart, answer those questions: *Yes! It's the greatest thing I could possibly do for them.*

You feel excited about your idea. You just can't wait to tell them. You call them together in a meeting and explain what you're going to

Chart 1
Personal Accountability
Inventory

What are some areas in which I need to be accountable?	What actions do I need to take?

do *for* your employees—then they call their own meeting to discuss what you're doing *to* them. Those are the facts of life.

Simply, people have been trained to resist our leadership. I don't believe this will ever be totally eliminated. The only chance we have of ever penetrating this barrier to communication—of overcoming this resistance to our leadership—is effective management on a daily basis. We must communicate to our employees that we do not want slaves. Rather, we want to work together in a mutual relationship designed so that each and everyone involved can fulfill his or her own needs.

The first step in establishing this type of a relationship is, as managers, being internalists, accepting personal accountability for our actions. Use Chart 1 to take an inventory of this in your management situation.

EVASIVE ACTION PLAN
To Avoid Fatal Error #1 by Building Personal Accountability

One of the Fortune Group's tools that has proved successful is "The Fortune Action Contract." After every session, most companies have the students complete it as a means of follow-up.

We have provided you with a contract for use with this program.

Instructions for Completing Action Contract

1. Under 1, write down the single most important idea you've heard during this session.
2. Under "How I will use it," write down:
   A. What you're going to do
   B. When you're going to do it
   C. With whom you're going to do it
3. What will be the benefit for you by using this idea?
4. In our sessions, we give the group a sixty-second preparation break, during which each person enters into a contract with the person next to him, someone else in the meeting, the facilitator of the session, or his manager. We suggest that you choose a person to share with.
   A. Tell that person what you're going to do
   B. Tell him how you're going to do it
   C. Tell him how it will benefit you
5. Make sure you write in the date of commitment and follow-up date for the person you have given this contract.

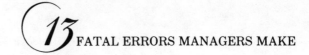

Fortune Action Contract

Because I feel this is the most important idea for me from this chapter, I make a firm commitment to use it within the next seven days.

1. *This is the single most important idea I got out of this chapter* that I can personally apply:

   _____

   _____

   _____

2. This is how I will use it:

   _____

   _____

   _____

3. What I will gain from its use:

   _____

   _____

   _____

4. Someone to share these ideas with:

   _____

   Date of commitment:_____

   Follow-up date:_____

FATAL
ERROR
2 Fail to Develop People

Management has a major purpose: *to provide for the continuation of the business over time, personnel change, and absence.* A properly managed business can continue successful operation over generations of employees and during the temporary or permanent absence of any given manager. This means that the operation under your supervision should function successfully while you are away for lunch, a seminar, a business trip, a vacation, or a short-term illness. Moreover, your permanent absence due to transfer to another position, retirement, poor health, or even death must not cripple the company. If it will, then you are neglecting your obligations as a manager.

Ineffective Management

Each time I conduct a seminar for a group of managers, I give those present three tests of their effectiveness as managers, one per break. The managers who have to call the office at lunch or on one of the two coffee breaks flunk my test, because any good manager can afford to leave the office for a single day without chaos ensuing.

It never fails to amaze me how many managers do not have to call the office but do anyway. We all know that if a problem is severe enough to genuinely deserve the manager's time, someone from the office will contact him or her. But we have trouble admitting why manag-

29

ers call: They need to feel needed, and few of us realize how strong that desire really is. Most of us get involved in management because of our ability to solve problems. The more we solve, the more people become dependent on us, and the more satisfaction we receive from problem solving. The smaller and simpler the problem, the more quickly we can solve it and feel the dual satisfaction of accomplishment and dependency.

Have you ever known a mother who was unable to cut the apron strings when little Johnny or Jenny got married or went away to college? The situation parallels that of managers who build dependency because of personal insecurity.

Most certainly there exist problems managers should solve. These are the unique ones, the difficulties no one could anticipate. Yet denying a subordinate the experience of solving his own routine problems denies him the opportunity for growth and, consequently, you fail him. When you call in to the office at 10:30 on a one- or two-day absence, you are saying, *I don't think you can stay out of trouble for even two hours without me there to watch over you.* Soon your employees' opinions of themselves become as low as they perceive yours to be.

As Mary Kay Ash says, instead managers must be gardeners of seeds of greatness:

> Every manager should understand that God has planted seeds of greatness in every human being. Each of us is important, and a good manager can bring these seeds to fruition! It's unfortunate that most of us go to our graves with our music still unplayed! It's been said that we use only 10 percent of our God-given ability, and that the other 90 percent is never tapped. . . .
>
> My experience with people is that they generally *do what you expect them to do!* If you expect them to perform well, they will; conversely, if you expect them to perform poorly, they'll probably oblige. I believe that average employees who try their hardest to live up to your high expectations of them will do better than above-average people with low self-esteem. Motivate your people to draw on that untapped 90 percent of their ability, and their level of performance will soar!

Those who cannot conquer the need for affection never build strong productive people; consequently, their teams remain weak. You cannot build a strong team on weak individuals. The test of a manager is not what he can do, rather it is what his people can do without him. Can they manage the routine tasks? Can they produce information suddenly called for by top management? Can they handle an equipment

ference between an actual experience and an imaginary experience that is repeated vividly. . . .

We're all talking to ourselves every moment of our lives, except during certain portions of our sleeping cycle. It comes automatically. We're seldom even aware that we're doing it. We all have a running commentary going on in our heads on events and our reactions to them. Many of our decisions are subconscious responses in our brain's right hemisphere and since they aren't expressed in words we get a gut-level feeling or some kind of visual or emotional response to what we see, hear, and touch. The left hemisphere verbally criticizes and approves what we consciously say and do. The left hemisphere also verbally abuses the subconscious reflexes caused by the right hemisphere. We see it on the tennis court and fairways every day. "Come on, you klutz, keep the ball in the court," "Keep your head down, you jerk." But it's not your partner across the net or in the foursome who's doing the criticizing. It's one of two partners in your own head! And the right hemisphere knows how to get even with the left. It puts the next drive in the lake, trips you on the tennis court, and gives you a headache and upset stomach just for openers!

The greatest challenge a person can face is the one that he has been trained for, assured he can meet, and given the opportunity of meeting. While no guarantee exists that the person will succeed every time, the challenge must face him. Nothing demotivates people more than lack of challenge. Like Lombardi, we must prepare our people and, from the sidelines, encourage them to put forth their best effort. Only in this way will we have time to grow ourselves.

Management Traps

The Activity Trap

Most of us in management feel we could do better by our people, if there just were more hours in the day, yet we have them all. We all get our full allotment of twenty-four per day, but when we look around, it seems as if some folks get thirty, while we have about eighteen. This leads us to the decision that we absolutely *have* to do a better job of managing our time. In that way, we can better assist our people. Unfortunately, we cannot manage time, for it is a dimension (like space) and we can only use it.

For example, have you had the experience of realizing one Friday afternoon that you no longer control your life? Determined to do something about the situation, you stop by a bookstore on the way home and buy a good book on self-management. You do not just read the book, you study it and take an oath: "If Monday is the last day of my life, I will make it count!"

At last you feel convinced that controlling your own time is a key element in developing those you manage.

You make those lists, and you set those priorities. You go to bed Sunday night with the warm glow of personal pride. On Monday you enter the office with a sense of purpose visible in your stride. You walk in as if you owned the world. Then before you can reach your office door, one of your subordinates stops you with the greeting, "Am I glad I caught you, because *we* have a problem."

You give the problem your immediate attention, as you should, but not having a ready solution, you say, "I'll have to get back to you on this."

What just happened? Before you reached the office, your subordinate had a problem. Now *you* have the problem. If you have ten people on your staff, they will be kind enough to supply you with 6 or 7 problems a day—that's at least 30 a week, 130 per month, 1,560 a year!

You see yourself as a take-charge manager. Aren't you doing what's right? Isn't solving problems your job? Yes and no. Certainly you should stop and listen to each employee's problem and counsel him as best you can, but no effective manager allows an employee to enter his or her office with a problem that the employee does not carry out the door upon leaving.

Remember, it's a Fatal Error not to develop your people. It's fatal to your time and their performance.

Somewhere, many managers have acquired an inverted view of how a business should be operated. Maybe it derives from the pride associated with being a take-charge guy and a tough troubleshooter. Most problem-solving managers at least seem to hold the notion that problems should be passed *up* the line, instead of *down* the line.

On the other hand, I believe that good managers are problem givers. Why bother to have a staff that cannot answer questions, face challenges, and solve problems you do not have time to handle?

In no way am I suggesting that you should ignore your subordinates. When one comes to you with a problem, we suggest the following course of action. STOP whatever you are doing. If you are filling out a report, don't just put down your pen, close the folder. LOOK at the person. Don't just look in his or her direction; study the face. LISTEN with your eyes as well as your ears. Not only make certain you clearly understand what problem the employee faces, you should also clearly understand the employee's reaction to it. Is he angry, fearful, irritated, or eager for the challenge? Once you know both the problem and the individual's attitude toward it, advise and counsel, but make certain that your subordinate carries the problem out of the office. If not, you will not be managing your staff—your staff will be managing you.

The One-and-a-Half-Generation-Pattern Trap

If you have any doubts as to the validity of building the strongest people possible, you need only note that the life span of most small businesses is one and a half generations. The documented pattern goes like this: A person starts a business, and it lasts through his or her working lifetime. It takes the successors only half a working generation to put the company out of business.

Why? Because those who start businesses tend to withhold all authority. By doing so, they guarantee that their companies will have short life spans. When you don't truly develop anyone to function in your place, you make no provision for the continuation of the business.

Whether you manage a small company or a section of a giant one, stop and think how well your people would do in your absence. Where would they most likely falter? Where would they encounter the greatest problems? If you make a list of these areas (see Chart 2), you have a list of your obligations as a manager: obligations to your people and to your company.

Do not look on this as a list of shortcomings on the part of anyone involved, rather as a list of goals for you to achieve. Keep it private, because if you drop the entire expectation on your employees at one time, they may crumble under its weight.

Some years back a newspaper reported the story of Frank Rickman. His mind simply rejected limitations. Among those was the belief that Georgia was no place for a ski resort. Frank had done his homework and knew that one sheltered area had all the right ingredients: hills, slopes, proximity to markets, and a low enough temperature. He not only believed in the feasibility of a resort, he had designed a spectacular lodge as the centerpiece of his proposed resort. Furthermore, he intended building it with local workers who had little or no experience building ski resorts. When he showed his basic concept and the geographically perfect spot to some visionary investors, the project started becoming a reality.

Months later, as Frank walked through the nearly completed building, with its complicated stairways and custom-built furnishings, asked how he had managed to accomplish such complex construction without a blueprint, except for the one in his head, he smiled and said, "In the beginning, I just told each crew member one thing at a time. When he said he could handle one job, then I'd give him another and another. But you can bet on this: If I'd even given these men a hint of how much I expected out of them in the beginning, they'd have quit before they

Chart 2
Goals for Employee Development

Areas in which my people would falter	Ways in which I can help them develop

Areas in which my people would encounter problems	How I can help them learn to solve these problems

started. But just look at them now! Now they believe they can handle anything."

Like Frank Rickman, you must not underestimate your people, because they will not exceed your expectations. And like Frank, you must not frighten your people by threatening them with the high expectations you know are possible, but which at first they may believe are too high!

The Electric-Fence Effect Trap

A friend named Wiley showed me about his farm. As we walked, we crested a knoll to face an electric fence, a single strand of wire marking the perimeter of a ten- or twelve-acre field. Wiley looked about, then placed one hand on the wire to steady himself, and stepped over. Seeing that he didn't get shocked, I followed his example and asked, "Why did you look around before stepping over that fence? And while I'm asking questions, what good is an electric fence if you don't have it turned on?"

Wiley smiled and said, "I was looking to see if any cattle were watching. I didn't want to put any ideas in their heads. Didn't you know that you don't have to leave an electric fence on all the time? Once they know it'll shock them, they graze right up to it and stop. See?" He pointed at the different heights of grass on the two sides of the wire.

Many of us treat our employees like cattle, so they react like cattle. Thinking that an old limitation still exists, they don't attempt to go further.

What powerless fences surround your people? How did they come into being in the first place? Situations that once existed in the marketplace may have built some of them. Others may have been built by you or some former manager. Any limitation your employees honor as if it were real, even though it no longer exists, will hold them back.

List those fences in Chart 3. Think about them. Show your people that those once very real limitations are now powerless to hold them back.

I am reminded of what Thomas Huxley said of education: "The greatest result of all education is developing the ability to do what needs to be done when it should be done, whether you like it or not." Of course, breaking habits and breaching the electric fences of personal fears and team inadequacies takes hard work. But the conscientious manager does what has to be done, whether or not he wants to and always works to develop people beyond their capabilities. Thereby he avoids Fatal Error #2.

Chart 3
Breaking the Power of Electric Fences

What unseen electric fences limit my staff?	How can I "turn off" the electricity?

EVASIVE ACTION PLAN
To Avoid Fatal Error #2 by Helping Individuals Develop Professionally

One of the Fortune Group's tools that has proved successful is "The Fortune Action Contract." After every session, most companies have the students complete it as a means of follow-up.

We have provided you with a contract for use with this program.

Instructions for Completing Action Contract

1. Under 1, write down the single most important idea you've heard during this session.
2. Under "How I will use it," write down:
   A. What you're going to do
   B. When you're going to do it
   C. With whom you're going to do it
3. What will be the benefit for you by using this idea?
4. In our sessions, we give the group a sixty-second preparation break, during which each person enters into a contract with the person next to him, someone else in the meeting, the facilitator of the session, or his manager. We suggest that you choose a person to share with.
   A. Tell that person what you're going to do
   B. Tell him how you're going to do it
   C. Tell him how it will benefit you
5. Make sure you write in the date of commitment and follow-up date for the person you have given this contract.

Fortune Action Contract

Because I feel this is the most important idea for me from this chapter, I make a firm commitment to use it within the next seven days.

1. *This is the single most important idea I got out of this chapter* that I can personally apply:

   _____

   _____

   _____

2. This is how I will use it:

_____

_____

_____

3. What I will gain from its use:

_____

_____

_____

4. Someone to share these ideas with:

_____

Date of commitment: _____

Follow-up date: _____

FATAL ERROR

3 Try to Control Results Instead of Influencing Thinking

It's self-evident that people act differently. Some are quite simply more productive than others. Regardless of the business arena, be it a typing pool, a data-processing department, a sales force, or a staff of nurses on a hospital floor, some produce more than others.

Especially in those fields where we may easily track results, such as the field of sales, managers observe this difference on a daily basis. In every sales force you'll have two salespeople in the same city, selling the same product or service to essentially the same clientele, and one of those salespeople will outproduce another—three or four to one. I think at some time in our careers, practically all of us in management have been frustrated and even a little bit mystified by this phenomenon.

We look at our people and ask, "What is the difference?" Certainly our higher performers do not look better than the others; neither are they more intelligent; and they don't appear to work any harder. Based on the years of experience I've had at the Fortune Group, I'm of the opinion that I have come to understand that difference.

What Makes People Successful?

People have written thousands of books about it, but I maintain that there is no great mystery as to why some people succeed

41

and others fail. The difference between the successful and nonsuccessful person is simple: *The successful person has developed the habit of doing the things unsuccessful people do not do.* Doubtless many factors influence success, but the basic reason most people get ahead is that they do good work.

Naturally, people succeed or fail based on their work habits, and most of us in management have recognized this for years. Yet work habits only form the tip of the iceberg. The challenge of increasing productivity is understanding what underlies the work habits and how and why people develop them.

Activity Is Not the Key

Because we recognize the importance of good work habits, those of us in management have spent untold amounts of energy attempting to help our people develop them. But often our well-meaning efforts have come to nothing. Why?

In many instances we failed because we concentrated only on the activity in which people should engage and on the results we desire. Knowing that performance emanates from behavior (or activity), we assumed that our employees would follow the progression shown in the first part of Illustration 1: activity, habits, results. But we have ignored the basic factors that influence our people to engage in activities and form habits and have experienced limited success.

Illustration 1
Productivity Chain Reaction

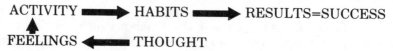

That does not mean a progression does not exist. The consistent performance and increased productivity every manager seeks *is* the final product of a chain reaction, but begins in the minds of our employees. Study the second part of Illustration 1: First, a thought must be accepted by the mind; that creates feelings; in turn feelings affect activity; rewarding activity leads to habits; in the end, habits generate results. Use this, and you will find a drastic change in productivity.

The chain reaction I have outlined works because *physical performance improves in direct proportion to mental discipline.* The Bible told us this many years ago in the verse "As a man thinks in his heart so is he" (*see* Proverbs 23:7). Our previous progression failed because it did not take into account the first two elements. Nothing is as powerful as thought. What goes into this software of our brain's computer controls what comes out.

Two examples from Denis Waitley's *The Double Win* illustrate this point:

> Robert had many reasons for marrying Pauline, and her cooking was in the top ten. It was, therefore, some time before he gathered the nerve to question a strange habit he had noticed: Each time she cooked a ham, she would first cut off both ends. When he finally asked her why, she answered, unhesitatingly, "That's the way my mother did it."
>
> Not totally satisfied, but unwilling to press her further, Bob waited until the next visit to the home of Pauline's parents. He posed the same question to Pauline's mother, and she replied cheerfully, "Why, that's the way *my* mom always cooked it."
>
> Determined to get to the bottom of the culinary mystery, Bob stopped by after work to visit Pauline's grandmother and casually broached the subject: "Why do you cut the ends off a ham before you bake it? I'm just curious," he smiled.
>
> She looked at him suspiciously and replied curtly, "Because my baking dish is too small!"
>
> Just like Robert's wife, we develop many of our behavior patterns through imitating and identifying with the values and attitudes modeled for us. . . .
>
> The same is true of any sport. I went to La Jolla High School with Gene Littler, the great PGA touring pro, who is generally acknowledged as having the "perfect" golf swing. As teenagers, Gene and I would go to the La Jolla Country Club for practice sessions. Gene would practice while I shagged golf balls. Almost every day, he would hit hundreds of balls to the 60, 75, 100, and 150-yard markers.
>
> As a very young boy, Gene had watched great golfers play. He had taken lessons from a great teaching professional and had learned the correct execution of each shot in the game. The great attitudinal skill that set Gene Littler's self-image thermostat high as a youth was his ability to recognize the effort required and his willingness to pay the price of "practicing winning" on and off the golf course. He knew the saying that applies to every skill, every sport, every business, and every high-performance situation in life:
>
> "You've got to learn the correct swing before you can play the game."
>
> As he mastered the game of golf by observing, imitating, and repeating the correct swings and strokes, he developed a high self-image which, in turn, resulted in a low handicap

and an incredible career as a professional. With a self-image built on competency and positive role models, he had a perfect navigational guidance computer during practice and tournament rounds of golf.

When, upon occasion, Gene Littler would hit a bad shot, I would overhear him making corrections with positive self-talk: "That's not like you; keep your head down and follow through." When I saw him hit an outstanding shot, right to the pin, I heard more positive self-talk: "Good, that's more like it. Now we're in the groove!"

By simply dealing with the external you cannot successfully inspire people to develop the habit patterns of success or increase their productivity. If this were possible, anyone could manage successfully, but most people cannot. Likewise, management needs accurate data and effective tracking systems, but you cannot manage people with numbers alone. Productivity increases as managers increasingly understand the human factor and effectively deal with attitudes, fears, motivational blocks, and the phantoms that lurk within the minds of people. Increased productivity is the direct result of thinking.

All too frequently we see news items concerning some tragedy attributed to "human error." When we read further—and between the lines—we usually learn that the fatal "human error" resulted from a poor work habit; someone neglected to perform a routine task. Also, the words *mechanical failure* may cover up sloppy work habits. Because it cannot speak in its defense, people blame the machine, instead of spotlighting the infrequency of thorough inspection that would have revealed a worn part or other clear warning signs. No wonder we have OSHA. Half its cumbersome mandates are nothing more than pathetic attempts to regulate good work habits, when the culprit is a lack of proper thinking.

The Key Questions

While we recognize that no one has the absolute answers when it comes to increasing productivity and developing the habit patterns of success, everyone who manages had better understand the questions. Two essential ones form the root of our thinking, when it comes to engaging in any activity long enough and consistently enough for that activity to become a habit, and determine our willingness to face new challenges and improve the quality of our work.

Can I Succeed?

When a person faces accepting a greater challenge—be it aiming for a higher goal, mastering a new skill, or increasing productivity—he first asks himself, *What are my chances of success?* If in his mind the answer comes back, *I can try, but I'm going to fail,* he simply will not try. An intelligent person expends effort and energy only when he can expect results and avoids engaging in acts of futility or apparent impossibility. In effect, when we ask ourselves this question, we rate ourselves against the task, based upon our perception as to its degree of difficulty.

When mentally rating ourselves, we do not use anything as simple as a numerical rating system. But we do work on a similar concept, and if we can understand this example you will have a clear idea how human motivation works. Suppose an employee rated himself numerically; he would assign a value to the task, saying, *I see the job my boss wants me to take on as a . . . ,* and he'd fill in a number from 1 to 5. Then he would assign himself a number in the same fashion. Now, if he saw himself as a 3 and the task as a 3, whew! It's tough. It may take everything he has, but he can handle it.

On the other hand, if he rates the task as a 1 or 2 and himself as a 3, it's a snap. Or if he gets a 3 and the task gets a 4 or 5, he cannot do it. He sees the job as too hard and will not even try. (*See* Illustration 2).

Even though we do not rate ourselves numerically, we do make the same kind of mental assessment of our worth and the difficulty of the job or situation we face. And we make many major decisions based upon such perceptions.

Illustration 2
Personal Motivation Rating
Degree of Difficulty

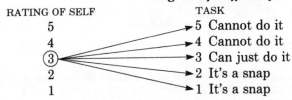

RATING OF SELF	TASK
5	5 Cannot do it
4	4 Cannot do it
③	3 Can just do it
2	2 It's a snap
1	1 It's a snap

Recently I met a young man who saw his objective as a snap. On my way to a management-training seminar in Cincinnati, Ohio, I left my home in Atlanta under less than ideal circumstances. When you travel as much as I do, you cherish your weekends with your family, but I had to fly that Sunday. In addition, the flight I had reservations on was not the nonstop one I had hoped to take, but landed in Lexington, Kentucky, on its way to my destination. Since one reason I live in Atlanta is because I can get a nonstop flight to practically any city in North America, I felt less than pleased.

Although I had booked coach, I planned to upgrade my seat to first class, but when I got to the airport, I found this was not possible. That capped off all my other disappointments, and to say the least, I was not in the best of spirits as I waited for my flight.

In the airport one man's size attracted my attention. He must have weighed at least 250 pounds. His wife, who was traveling with him, was *really* a big woman, outweighing him by at least 50 pounds. Even though they stood next to a man much larger than I, they literally dwarfed him.

From their manner I thought perhaps they had been drinking. I thought, *Oh, no, certainly they won't be seated next to me.* Then I began to pray, "Lord, deliver me from this!"

As I found my seat on the plane, a center one in coach, I looked to the right and left and felt relief that both remained vacant. Breathing a sigh, I pulled out a book and began to relax. Just as the plane prepared to move away from the jetway, I looked up and saw the young couple, bumping people on both sides of the aisle and headed in my direction.

She moved into my row of seats and sat on my left. He took his place on my right. They sort of overflowed onto me. Burrowing my nose closer into my book, I assumed they'd realize that I wasn't reading, but didn't want to be bothered. After all, no one can see with a book that close, and everyone knows, when you do that, when your real aim is to avoid conversation. I thought I had successfully accomplished my purpose. But no sooner had the plane left the ground—the no-smoking sign was not yet off—when the woman turned to me and said, "Hey, mister!" I pretended not to have heard. In a louder voice she said, "Hey, mister!"

Timidly I responded, "Yes?"

She said, "Do you know you're flying with a million-dollar salesman?"

"What do you mean?"

"I'm Louise," she introduced herself.

He turned to me and put a hand as big as a ham in my face and said, "Hi! I'm Hector."

Proudly his wife told me, "Hector's a million-dollar salesman. We've been to Bermuda, and he won the trip!" This couple were two of the most delightful young people I've ever met.

Hector sold farm supplies. He had won, based on his productivity for the past year, a trip to Bermuda for him and his wife. What made them so exciting and so much fun is that these kids would never have made that trip if Hector had not won it. I so much enjoyed my conversation with them and their enthusiasm. Having gotten acquainted, jokingly I told Louise, "You know, Louise, this is Sunday afternoon. You and Hector are coming back from Bermuda, and I know there'll be a trip offered by your company next year. So you had better make sure that Hector gets an early start tomorrow morning so that you can win the trip next year."

Hector calmly stated, "It's Lake Tahoe. We'll be there."

I said, "What?"

"It's Lake Tahoe. We'll be there."

"What does your company require for you to earn the trip to Lake Tahoe?"

"All they want is a twenty-seven percent increase in my territory. I'll get a forty percent increase."

Hector and Louise *will be* in Lake Tahoe, because to him the twenty-seven percent increase is a snap.

I'll assure you that in that same company, other salespeople will not make the trip to Lake Tahoe, people who will not even face the challenge or really put forth their very best effort to earn that trip, because in their minds a twenty-seven percent increase is a 5, and they see themselves only as 3s. It lies beyond them, and in their minds they cannot accomplish it (*see* Chart 4).

On a daily basis, you and I as managers face a major challenge of reforming the attitude of those on our staff who see doing the job, or at least doing the job at a high level of productivity, as being beyond them. You and I may know that the job is not that difficult, but that does not matter. It makes no difference what we think. What the employee thinks is the only thing that is important.

How do we influence our employees' thinking? Not by trying to sell them on the fact that they can do the job more easily than they think. You, as a manager, can tell the person it's just not that hard, but you're wasting time, battling against the big guns of contradiction that fire back (audibly or otherwise). "Baloney," the 3 says. "You haven't been in the field in the last five years. What do you know?" "You were working in the West Coast plant, and this is the East Coast." "You never had to deal with today's production quotas, competition, interest rates." "My territory is different."

Words alone will not change the person's perception as to the degree of difficulty of the task. You see, our only real hope lies in changing that person's perception of self. Imagine the self-doubting employee as a woodcutter, leaning on his trusty double-bladed ax as the boss says, "Starting tomorrow, I want you to fell twice as many trees per day as in the past." The chances of the woodcutter replying "No problem" are too small to calculate.

On the other hand, consider the possible response if the boss adds, "Here's a chain saw, and I'll teach you how to use it." The addition of the proper tools suddenly changes the concepts of one's ability. The tools of improved performance include new marketing plans, new systems, new equipment, and more often than not, additional mental tools—new information, new training, helping the person develop increased skills that will cause him to believe that he can perform at a higher level.

Chart 4
Productivity Chain-Reaction
Example

Let's use the story of Hector as an example of how this chain reaction works, compared to a fictitious salesman we'll call Fred, who is not properly motivated. Both are told, "If you effect a twenty-seven percent increase in sales in your territory, you'll earn a trip to Lake Tahoe."

THOUGHT
> FRED: *That's a 5, and I'm only a 3.*
> HECTOR: *That's only a 3, and I'm a 5.*

FEELINGS
> FRED: *I can never do it.*
> HECTOR: *I can do 40%, instead of 27%.*

BEHAVIOR
> FRED: Sells at about the usual pace.
> HECTOR: Increases activity to increase sales.

RESULTS
> FRED: Sells less than 27% increase and does not go to Lake Tahoe.
> HECTOR: Increases sales by 40% and goes to Lake Tahoe.

Fred needs to be managed differently from Hector. His manager needs to see inside Fred's thoughts and help him become an achiever.

Where Is the Value to Me?

The second question people ask themselves when faced with a new challenge is *Where is the value to me?* If they perceive greater value in performing the task, they will perform. On the other hand, if they see greater value in not performing the task, they will, quite simply, refuse to do so.

When I say people ask the question *Where is the value to me?* I am not referring to money. Understandably, if we will not pay people, they will not work. People do not work for money per se, unless they face extreme financial pressure. The person under enough financial stress will do practically anything, no matter how distasteful to him, for the period of time necessary to acquire enough money to get the financial pressure off his back. When the pressure no longer exists, he will not continue to engage in these activities.

When one asks, *Where is the value to me?* he really means, *Where is the self-esteem?* More than anything else you and I seek self-esteem. We will engage in any activity long enough for it to become a habit only if we can derive self-esteem from our action. We will put intense interest in any activity and take pride in higher levels of performance only if we can derive self-esteem from doing so. I understand that in 1981, a year with one of the highest unemployment rates in recent history, over 10 million Americans quit their jobs. Let me assure you, they did not quit because of money. They quit because they were unable to derive self-esteem from that job.

A young friend of mine, I'll call him Dick, with only six months' management experience, learned the hard way about causing an employee to feel unimportant and denying a person self-esteem. His mistake cost him a most valuable associate. The circumstances were a little unusual, but I believe situations like this occur in businesses daily.

Dick belongs to a small firm that has experienced tremendous growth over the past several years. One of the most valuable employees, Gloria, joined the firm on a part-time basis, handling their data processing, working half days. She really preferred this schedule because of family commitments. However, due to the growth of the business, her job soon required working a full forty-hour week and even more. In spite of the conflicts this produced with her family commitments, she continued to hold down the job because she knew how important it was to the company. The self-esteem she derived from being an integral part of the team enabled her to withstand the family pressures. Dick made a management mistake when the family pressures were at their greatest, which cost him this most valuable employee. A series of circumstances involving illness on the part of two members of the four-person support team and a commitment for a third to be out of town evolved, so that Gloria was the only member of that support staff present on a particularly hectic day.

When she arrived at the office that morning, realizing the situation and work load, Gloria went to Dick and requested that he bring in temporary help to answer the phones and assist with typing. Dick, who had been charged with the responsibility of keeping costs under control, sought to avoid increased costs by responding, "That's not necessary. We [meaning himself and the sales force] will all pitch in and help." Unfortunately, he failed to follow through. He did not ask the team to assist Gloria before he left the office for an all-day meeting. Gloria, quite naturally, felt unimportant, ignored, devalued. His actions destroyed her ability to derive self-esteem from the job. This straw, along with the family pressures, broke the camel's back. She resigned the following morning. I do not intend to be too rough on Dick, but I'm attempting to illustrate that his failure to be in touch with the internal needs of his staff cost his company greatly.

Deriving Self-Esteem

People answer the question, *Where is the value to me?* in essentially the same way that they form their answer to the question *What are my chances of success?* That is, in viewing the job itself or the activities that make up the job, they assign the job or task a value (1 through 5) and themselves a value (1 through 5). From an esteem standpoint, if they see themselves as a 3 and the job to be done as a 3, they can and will derive self-esteem from it. Their pride in the situation enables them to perform at high levels of productivity over an extended period of time. If the number they assign the job is higher than theirs, they will strive to attain to it.

Illustration 3
Personal Motivation Rating
Self-esteem

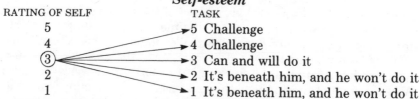

RATING OF SELF	TASK
5	5 Challenge
4	4 Challenge
③	3 Can and will do it
2	2 It's beneath him, and he won't do it
1	1 It's beneath him, and he won't do it

On the other hand, as they perceive themselves to be a 3 and the task to be performed as a 1 or 2, it appears at best mundane and more often than not seems beneath them. They have little sense of self-esteem, and they either will not do the job, or if they take it on at all, do so halfheartedly. (*See* Illustration 3.)

This affects the productivity of people at all levels. A lot of managers suffer from *executivitis* and find it practically impossible to do the nitty-gritty, unglamorous tasks involved in management. A seasoned secretary, called on to serve temporarily as a receptionist, finds it a blow to her ego. Territory realignments and reclassification of grades or job titles are a put-down to many. In each case the price is paid in productivity.

Managers of salespeople face this challenge every day, because to some extent we all believe that the job of sales lacks status. For years they've rated various professions on status at the college level. Medicine invariably ranks at the top, and sales is always at or near the bottom.

Only about 5 percent of the young men and women who graduate with degrees in business will condescend to go into sales. However, by the time these people reach age thirty, over 75 percent of them are involved in selling in some form. Furthermore, many do it poorly, because they have been taught that selling is a form of failure, and they feel *ashamed* of their profession. Since no sales manager can wait on the educational system to embrace and champion the realities of life, an effective sales manager provides an unlearning/relearning process that alters attitudes and boosts self-esteem, as well as develops skills.

We at the Fortune Group have seen this lack of esteem in selling most graphically illustrated in the banking industry. With deregulation, financial institutions, if they are to survive, must become marketers and sellers of financial services. We have had a firsthand opportunity to view the frustration facing the senior management of financial institutions, generated by their futile attempts to train bankers to become salespeople, when if they had any desire or could have derived any self-esteem from being salespeople, they would never have gone to work for a bank.

In the mental rating process, where self-esteem is concerned, if a person sees himself as a 3 and the job as a 5, he aspires to do it. He is turned on by it. It provides him with a reason for living and, in some cases even dying. Every martyr for every cause has been willing to martyr himself because he felt the cause was greater than the individual. When people see themselves as 3s and the job as a 5, they will fight tanks in the street with their bare hands.

In management we don't need people with this devotion, but we do need people who deeply believe in what they do, who understand the importance of their job, and who take great pride in what they do.

EVASIVE ACTION PLAN
To Avoid Fatal Error #3 by Influencing Thinking Instead of Controlling Results

One of the Fortune Group's tools that has proved successful is "The Fortune Action Contract." After every session, most companies have the students complete it as a means of follow-up.

We have provided you with a contract for use with this program.

Instructions for Completing Action Contract

1. Under 1, write down the single most important idea you've heard during this session.
2. Under "How I will use it," write down:
   A. What you're going to do
   B. When you're going to do it
   C. With whom you're going to do it
3. What will be the benefit for you by using this idea?
4. In our sessions, we give the group a sixty-second preparation break, during which each person enters into a contract with the person next to him, someone else in the meeting, the facilitator of the session, or his manager. We suggest that you choose a person to share with.
   A. Tell that person what you're going to do
   B. Tell him how you're going to do it
   C. Tell him how it will benefit you
5. Make sure you write in the date of commitment and follow-up date for the person you have given this contract.

Fortune Action Contract

Because I feel this is the most important idea for me from this chapter, I make a firm commitment to use it within the next seven days.

1. *This is the single most important idea I got out of this chapter* that I can personally apply:

   _____

   _____

   _____

2. This is how I will use it:

   _____

   _____

   _____

3. What I will gain from its use:

_____

_____

_____

4. Someone to share these ideas with:

_____

Date of commitment: _____

Follow-up date: _____

FATAL ERROR

4

Join the Wrong Crowd

In telling you not to join the wrong crowd, I'm not talking about corporate gamesmanship but about fostering the right attitude. Let me explain.

The Fatal-Pronoun Disease

In traveling about the country to work with all types of companies, I have learned to spot certain danger signals. Certain words and phrases let me know a manager stands on dangerous ground. I pay particular attention to the use of pronouns, because only one pronoun should be used when speaking of any part of your organization: *we*.

One large organization's management team had expressed a need for a comprehensive efficiency analysis. The company's president, several other key executives, and I met with the line managers. All expressed concern that the members of the work force seemed uncertain, in view of recent changes, as to where they should place their concentration and how to properly analyze their progress. After many hours of hard work, we produced a tool designed to track the work flow and most productive activities. Everyone left the meeting agreeing that the new system could do the job.

The paperwork was quick copied, and the managers headed out to meet with their staff members. I had the opportunity to observe one of the managers present the analysis to his people, without his being aware of my presence. He walked to the front of the room, held up the papers, and said, "I've just come back from one of *their* meetings downtown. I don't know how *they* expect *us* to get any work done if *we* have to spend all *our* time in meetings. Anyway, have these filled out and on my desk by tomorrow morning."

I knew then that the company was ailing from the pronoun disease and that manager was the major carrier of the lethal germ.

If you hear yourself or some other manager use the pronoun *they,* warning signals should begin to flash. Listen very carefully to learn to whom the person refers. Who is *they?* No *they* should exist within an organization. But if there is one, *it must be the people you manage.*

When a manager refers to senior management as *they,* he is not mentally affiliating with management and does not see himself as part of the management team; therefore he drives a wedge between these employees and the rest of the organization. He fails management, and most important, he fails his people as well. All become victims of the pronoun disease.

Contagious Conditions

In a later chapter, I will show how attitudes are highly contagious and can sweep through your staff. You will want to encourage this when the attitudes are positive, but negative ones are killers.

These become especially dangerous when the attitudes spring out of the pronoun disease. All managers need to know about the following ones and look out for them.

The Loyalty Challenge

This comes in several forms, but the key is any form of challenge to the manager's loyalty to the company and its management. Look at these examples:

THE SIDELINES TROUBLEMAKER.   Since we are all human, we may easily become the target of some malcontent unwilling to remain alone in his disenchantment. Every corporation or business seems to include one staff member who tries to split management into warring factions. In order to do this, he must enlist recruits—and you will do nicely. But watch out, because such a person usually has no intention of jumping into the battle; he wants someone else to take the risks while he stands on the sidelines. When you begin to hear variations of "Let's you and them fight," be assured that you are about to be led into slaughter by someone with no plans to share your unhappy fate.

THE DEATH-MARCH TROUBLEMAKER.   Others invite you to join them on their own death march. Even though it appears obvious that their tactics cannot succeed, such persons expend much energy in what

Chart 5
Combating the Fatal Pronoun Disease

When have I used fatal pronouns?	Why?	How can I stop?

When have I heard others using fatal pronouns?	Why?	How can I best respond?

seems a fruitless cause. If, as I said before, people will not attempt a task that cannot be accomplished, you may well ask, "Why, then, would anyone attempt to instigate a palace revolt if he or she didn't believe it could be successful?"

The answer is that a successful revolt may not be the person's goal. He may simply be griping, something that has become a habit for him, yet plan to do nothing about his areas of complaint. Or he may have such a warped perspective that making trouble for those he dislikes becomes the goal, with no regard given to the consequences. Perhaps he wants to get fired in order to have someone to blame for his failure. No one, internalist or externalist, ever tries to achieve that which he does not feel he can accomplish.

THE GOOD-CAUSE TROUBLEMAKER. One of the most seductive appeals to some managers is to be a crusader for *their* people against corporate policy, goals, and objectives. Whether the person inviting you to such an improper affiliation holds a job as a fellow manager or an employee, you must decline. Even if you secretly agree with the person's complaints, keep that to yourself. If doing so is too hard a task, then you should seek employment elsewhere—and perhaps in some capacity other than management.

Combat the fatal-pronoun disease by making yourself aware of ways in which you and others have fallen in the trap. Use Chart 5 to identify problem areas.

Making Loyalty Work for You

The high expectations of loyalty placed upon all managers may help you or hinder you, depending upon your own attitudes and actions. Let's look at the importance and role of loyalty in a manager's job from your point of view and that of your company. What makes loyalty so crucial to a business? Does it mean that you must agree with everything your company does? How does this work in the marketplace?

From the side of those who hire, John Wareham points out in his book *Secrets of a Corporate Headhunter* that loyalty is the key to both getting a job and keeping it:

> The key to loyalty, whether you're recruiting an executive or making a friend, is in finding that *common ideal.* . . .
> *Look for loyalty to your cause.* One man's freedom fighter is another's terrorist, but whatever side of the fence you find yourself on, you can always admire loyalty, even in an enemy. The sort of admiration that you'd feel for the old woman who, in time of war, started out with a poker when the enemy was approaching. When asked what she could do

> with her rather mild weapon, she replied, "I can show them which side I am on."
>
> Karl Menninger would have understood exactly what she meant—he gave a nice definition of loyalty: "Loyalty means not that I *agree* with everything you say or that I believe you are always right. Loyalty means that I share a common ideal with you and that, regardless of minor differences, we fight for it, shoulder to shoulder, confident in one another's good faith, trust, constancy, and affection."

He shows that loyalty does not mean you must always share your superior's point of view, anymore than your staff must agree with yours. Nevertheless, there must exist a chain of command and respect for the structure. When you treat these lightly, you will cause trouble for both yourself and those for whom you work, and things will no longer move smoothly. This is why the wise manager seeks his closest friendships outside the company, because he thereby avoids the great temptation to establish improper affiliations in the workplace.

An example of a situation that proves these truths is the firing of Douglas MacArthur by Harry Truman. When he did this, President Truman stated that he had not terminated the general's career because of their differences of opinion or because of personal insults, but because he had lost respect for the office of the president. That could not be tolerated.

You can handle such differences of opinion in a better way. As I wrote this book, two acquaintances of mine found themselves locked in an awkward situation. The president of a company (I'll call him Jack) made a decision to withdraw successful marketing efforts from two small-profit markets and gamble on establishing a strong foothold in another market that promised higher profits and far greater competition. His sales manager (I'll call him Tom) is strongly opposed to the move and feels it may ruin the company. The two have discussed the matter privately numerous times and still do not share a mutual opinion. Nonetheless, Tom put his total effort behind making Jack's plan a success. He has communicated that to his entire sales team. At the same time, he is looking for another position. Simply put, Tom understands the importance of proper affiliations.

Jack told me that he knows he could lose Tom over this difference of opinion; however he will write Tom the strongest letter of recommendation anyone could wish, because of Tom's respect for his authority and the corporate structure.

On the other hand, if Tom had chosen to create dissension among the troops over the matter and allow neither plan to enjoy total support, I can assure you that the only letter written would be one of dismissal.

Which man's opinion is correct? Beats me; I only know that both Jack and Tom understand and respect the importance of unity of effort in business, and Tom has shown loyalty in his actions.

Promoting Beyond the Confidence Level

One of the major causes of improper affiliations in managers is the common practice of promoting from within the ranks. The following happens. Someone is a top performer in the field, and a promotion seems the logical reward, so the company calls that person in to manage.

While I believe in promoting from within the ranks, it has to be done in a manner that retains a competence and a confidence level on the part of the newly named manager. He certainly should understand the problems of the field force, but does he also understand the problems of management? Very often he does not.

Too few firms recognize this situation and attempt to solve it by making the potential managers go through training courses. The classroom is an excellent first step; however, it does not do enough. We might compare just attending formal classes and seminars to trying to train a person to swim without letting him go near the water until the day you throw him in the deep end, where he sinks, swims, or barely manages to tread water. You can lose a lot of potentially good swimmers this way.

A company needs to provide intermediary steps to make certain some potentially fine managers don't go under. The size of the company or division will affect the form they take; however the principle remains the same in all cases. Give the manager-to-be new responsibilities by degrees. He or she can assist a current manager or fill in during his absence. Larger companies may create an assistant manager's position. All cases should include a careful feeding out of responsibility and authority.

In some instances, management will discover that the person has no real aptitude for the new position. If that is so, the person should be eased back into what he does best. And it must be done in a way that the wind is not taken out of his sails. No one profits when a company promotes a productive person to become a poor manager and later throws him back to flounder, with destroyed self-esteem, as "one of the troops."

By gradually moving people into management, they become better qualified for promotion and develop a mental affiliation with management. This process holds true for any division within a company. The top engineer, chemist, writer, researcher, or whatever may or may not be excellent management material. If not, leave the person at the top of his capabilities and financially compensate him on the basis of his contributions to the company's success. For an engineering firm to turn its resident genius into a poor manager simply because the only higher salary slots are at the management level is folly of the highest order. Nonetheless, all types of businesses make similar costly promotions all the time.

THE RIGHT STUFF.   When a person has a MANAGER label slapped on him, he will not automatically change his mind-set. He will still consider management as "they" if he does not feel comfortable with the new label. The person made of nothing but the right stuff can make the transition completely on his own. Most need some boost, in the form of training and a gradual transition of responsibilities. If the company does not provide assistance, it then becomes the newly named manager's personal responsibility to make the transition on his or her own. It can be done by watching pronouns and stopping oneself any time separatist-type thoughts begin to form, by not teaming up with malcontents, and by not giving in to the temptation to be an externalist and lay the blame on others.

You can avoid Fatal Error #4 by making sure that you and your people keep the right attitudes and affiliations to carry out management's role and responsibility.

EVASIVE ACTION PLAN
To Avoid Fatal Error #4 by Encouraging the Right Attitudes

One of the Fortune Group's tools that has proved successful is "The Fortune Action Contract." After every session, most companies have the students complete it as a means of follow-up.

We have provided you with a contract for use with this program.

Instructions for Completing Action Contract

1. Under 1, write down the single most important idea you've heard during this session.
2. Under "How I will use it," write down:
   A. What you're going to do
   B. When you're going to do it
   C. With whom you're going to do it
3. What will be the benefit for you by using this idea?
4. In our sessions, we give the group a sixty-second preparation break, during which each person enters into a contract with the person next to him, someone else in the meeting, the facilitator of the session, or his manager. We suggest that you choose a person to share with.
   A. Tell that person what you're going to do

    B. Tell him how you're going to do it

    C. Tell him how it will benefit you

5. Make sure you write in the date of commitment and follow-up date for the person you have given this contract.

Fortune Action Contract

Because I feel this is the most important idea for me from this chapter, I make a firm commitment to use it within the next seven days.

1. *This is the single most important idea I got out of this chapter* that I can personally apply:

    _____

    _____

    _____

2. This is how I will use it:

    _____

    _____

    _____

3. What I will gain from its use:

    _____

    _____

    _____

4. Someone to share these ideas with:

    _____

Date of commitment:_____

Follow-up date:_____

FATAL
ERROR

5 Manage Everyone the Same Way

The manager who tries to manage everyone on his staff the same way, using only one technique, can prepare himself for disappointments. He will never be successful (and probably will wonder why). The successful manager grasps ahold of the essential differences in the personalities of those on his staff and, aware of their strengths and weaknesses, manages them as individuals.

Weak Management Techniques

First let's look at the problem. Here are some of the pitfalls managers may fall into because of their own weaknesses or lack of knowledge.

The Management Mantle

This flaw originates in the manager's view of his own position. Frequently it has been taught to him by others in management, who have told him he must portray some sort of "proper" management role. These individuals get up in the morning and put on their role as if they were donning a mantle. In some circles it's characterized by a cold accountant's smile; in others it's a hardy, hail-fellow-well-met sales manner. In most places their different manners exist, according to rank.

This attitude and the harping on rank that accompanies it do more to hurt a company than help it. So often it backfires anyway, telling employees that the manager does not feel certain he is up to the task and needs all the trappings he can muster in order to seem capable of his role.

Group Management

Many managers attempt to deal with a mass of staff at one time, in an effort to avoid threatening personal contact. Such poor methods take many forms.

MANAGEMENT BY STAFF MEETING. Mantle managers by the score fall into this trap. They honestly believe that their weekly or monthly staff meeting provides their greatest management opportunity. During this time they may train, exchange information, do some problem solving, and even inspire the staff, but they do *not* effectively manage.

INNOCENT-GUILTY ATTACK. Managers who wish to avoid confrontation by firing off hot memos or railing at everyone from behind the stars and bars of the staff meeting attack the innocent along with the guilty. It doesn't matter that your words are followed by ". . . And you guilty ones know what I'm talking about." Chances are that the guilty ones aren't listening, while the rest leave the meeting depressed and unmotivated.

NAME THAT NAME. Just as bad, if not worse, is publicly naming the person who is out of line. It accomplishes only a widening of the communications gap between you and that employee, along with losing the respect of the rest of the staff.

Mary Kay Ash describes the results of such group management this way:

> It's inexcusable for a manager to chastise someone in the presence of others. Yet I've seen managers who while addressing a group will single out one person for criticism. I can't imagine anything more demoralizing.
>
> It's not only self-defeating to criticize someone in front of others, it's also downright cruel. A plant manager, for instance, should never berate a foreman in front of assembly-line workers. Imagine the repercussions if a manager spot-checking quality control were to shout at a foreman, "Look what you're allowing your people to put through, Joe. You know the company can't accept this kind of inferior quality. You're running a third-rate operation here. Just keep it up and you won't be around here very long."
>
> Not only does such action create bitter resentment, but

everyone present becomes embarrassed and insecure. A "Will I be next?" atmosphere is created, everyone feels threatened, and productivity suffers. In this case the workers may have begun to question the ability of their foreman, thereby reducing *his* effectiveness as a manager. Moreover, the foreman's self-esteem would have been badly bruised, making him unsure and hesitant. Although the poor quality of work may have been a very real problem, the manager's clumsy handling of the matter could have only aggravated the situation. Rather than publicly attacking the foreman, the manager should have privately discussed the issue. I think this would have enhanced the probability of solving a legitimate production problem and it would have preserved the morale of both the foreman and his workers. All parties, including the company, would have then profited.

Management is a one-to-one proposition. If you say something to an audience of one, no one doubts who you aim at. Furthermore, such confrontation provides you with an opportunity to learn the root of the problem.

Why Managers Try to Manage Through Groups

If this technique proves so ineffective, why do so many people try it?

Some lazy managers are simply unwilling to take the time to do their jobs properly and attempt to do a week's worth of work at a meeting. They do not fool their staff for a second. Others have never mastered the basic skill of looking another person in the eyes and simply saying what's on their minds. For them the back wall of the meeting room is the focus of their management efforts. Still others see the staff meeting as an expression of power, as in the following example.

I sat in on a monthly sales meeting where the general manager held sixty-six people captive while he dissected the long-distance telephone bill. An hour and fifteen minutes into the meeting, he was still in front of the group saying, "Next, we have this call to Fayetteville on the twenty-fourth. Somebody made it. Who?"

A man answered, "I made it."

He lied.

He never made the call, but he would have said *anything* to get out of that room! I almost admitted to making it myself.

The company had only one reasonable choice when the bill arrived: Pay it and shut up. After paying the bill, the company could establish some sort of control (such as one of the long-distance services that codes calls according to caller and client).

But ask youself this: Why would a person in charge of an office where the cost of keeping the front door open for business is several thousand dollars per hour tie up the entire operation over a $1.67 phone call? He certainly wasn't saving money. Was he setting standards of operation? I don't think so. In my view, he enjoyed having a gloriously satisfying time playing tyrant at the expense of the company. The man did not get the respect he wanted and took this monthly opportunity to attack everyone. His ego was bruised—maybe in childhood, who knows?—but he insisted on using a group meeting to demonstrate his power. So all he got was a further loss of respect.

One day I watched a man with an extensive background in military training conduct a training session for salespeople. Although he had never worked as a salesman, he was technically competent to conduct this product-knowledge technical meeting. Roughly thirty minutes after the meeting's start, the back door of the room opened, and I saw a great shock of silver hair. A big, handsome man in his mid-sixties entered. When he realized he was late, he scrunched up, making himself as small as possible, and tiptoed over to a chair. He prepared to sit down when the man running the meeting stopped him with the question, "What is your name, sir?"

"Peters, sir. I'm awfully sorry I'm late."

"Mr. Peters, what time was this meeting called for?"

"Nine o'clock, sir."

"Mr. Peters, do you have a military background?"

"Yes, I do, sir."

"Mr. Peters, in the military, if you had arrived at nine-thirty for a nine o'clock meeting, what would have happened?"

With that Peters drew himself up to his full height and smiled, "When I entered, everyone would have stood, saluted, and said, 'Good morning, sir.' "

Peters was a retired general! The major lesson of the day was learned by the man in charge of the meeting: Before you do it, you had best know whom you are about to jump. Maybe he also learned something about trusting and respecting the responsibility of his employees.

If someone comes into a meeting late, assume that that person has a reason for doing so. If someone leaves early, assume that the reason is perfectly acceptable. However, if a person is chronically late or habitually leaves before you adjourn meetings, get with that person one-to-one, talk to him individually, and avoid attacking him in front of the group.

Consider the above story: When the manager in charge attacked Peters, he wasn't trying to help Peters or the group. He attacked Peters for one reason: That late arrival affronted his ego. We attack someone because we aren't being treated with the importance and respect we feel we deserve. When we let our egos get out in front of us, we attack our people and definitely fail them—and ourselves.

In graphic contrast to the Norfolk incident, one day I attended a meeting where Don Kehoe, president of the Coca-Cola Company, made a presentation that was being filmed by the Fortune Group's production company. In the middle of the presentation, two men walked in. Mr. Kehoe interjected, "Come on in, fellows, you're late for the door prize," and continued his presentation without a falter.

Afterwards someone asked if he wanted to reshoot the interrupted portion. "Why?" he asked. "If my executives are late, they have a reason for it."

Such mature management recognizes that people who attempt managing in groups lose command and mismanage, rather than manage. Now let's look at some good management techniques.

Proper People Management

Certainly proper "paper administration" forms a part of management, but privately most of us will admit that a $1,500-a-month clerical person could do a better job with the paperwork than most managers. Yet for that kind of money you will never hire someone who can effectively deal with people. So make good people management one of your goals using these ideas that will help you treat each of your staff as an individual.

DEAL WITH EMPLOYEES ONE-TO-ONE.   Earlier we saw the flaws in trying to reach one person by pointing out the trouble to the whole staff. A wise manager makes an effort to call aside the person whom he wants to correct, so that problems may be dealt with on a one-to-one basis.

If you manage people who do not punch a time clock, your best opportunity with the morning person is when he or she arrives. This may require your being at the office to greet her at seven. You may need to swing by at night or pick up the phone at ten or eleven to work with the night person. With another the best approach is to stop by his desk and say, "Let's go grab a hot dog for lunch," or to pour two cups of coffee, go over to him, and say, "Let's talk." A game of golf, a get-together over breakfast, even in your office, if you don't hide behind your desk, may also provide opportunities. Whatever the situation, it should be just the two of you.

BE AWARE, BE AVAILABLE.   You can best fulfill these commands if you place your office in a position near the lobby, parking lot, or the hall. In doing this you will nip many management problems in the bud. Instead of ducking in the back, to hide yourself behind a protective barrier of paperwork and a closed door, you will spot problems and prevent someone from going home and staring at failure, written on the ceiling, all night long. When employees arrive angry, dejected, or tense, you may steer them into your office for a talk, avoiding their getting back to the staff and spreading poison. You will have scores of opportunities to help the people who depend on you, if you don't lose yourself to the easier, more exact science of paperwork, and remember that you were hired to deal with people.

Different Strokes

I hear frustrated managers declare a particular person a lost cause when the guy does not respond in exactly the same way another did to a particular technique. When one manager asked if I agreed that he should terminate a certain employee, I asked him to show me his key ring. Puzzled, he complied. I selected a key and asked, "What does this open?"

"The door to my station wagon."

"Will it also unlock your wife's car?"

"No. Of course not."

"Well, it's a perfectly good key. We know it works. Why don't you junk her car and get another one that will open with this station-wagon key?"

Obviously he has another key that operates her car, just as another technique is the key to getting the second employee to respond in the desired way. A technique that serves well with one individual may be useless when used on another.

Good management involves selection as well as application.

Also remember that once you have a key that causes a particular individual to open up, turn on, and go, you can usually depend on that key to work over and over again when you deal with that individual.

The Four Managerial Styles

All effective managers use a mixture of these major managerial styles or approaches, varying them to match the employee's needs, emotions, or the situation.

1. AUTOCRATIC MANAGEMENT.   As the word *autocratic* implies, this manager draws from his own strength. He says, "Do it this way...." "I said so...." "If you work here, this is the way it will be handled."

Two factors determine whether or not autocratic management works:

      1. The circumstances (the conditions at the moment)
      2. Who is being managed

Let's be realistic. At times autocratic management alone will get the job done. When the bullets fly, you do not call a meeting and solicit opinions. No. Someone takes charge and directs the entire operation; circumstances demand it.

Mike Vance, former Disney "imagineer," tells the story of a manager overseeing some employees leading tired trolley horses out of the traffic on Main Street in Disneyland. The crush of the crowd began to panic the horses. He took charge, giving commands to the crowd and the handlers and got the horses to their stable by an alternate route. Then, when the horses were safely out of the way, he turned to the handlers and said, "We've got a problem. How can we get tired horses out through crowded streets at closing time?" Clearly one situation demanded autocratic leadership and the later moment demanded democratic problem solving.

The other factor in autocratic management's effectiveness is the person you manage. You cannot manage some people in this way. Even if they know your chosen method is the only realistic approach, they will not budge; they would die first. Privately, one-to-one, employ another method.

The opposite is true with someone else. You are very new to management if you have not met the person who will fail to hear anything you say unless you, figuratively speaking, bust him right between the eyes with it. If an individual only responds to that form of management, the effective manager uses no other on him. Anything else he probably considers weakness.

2. BUREAUCRATIC MANAGEMENT. This means management by the rule book. The policy and procedural manual calls cadence. As with autocratic management, when it works, it's good. When it doesn't, it's bad. However, I feel we often overwork bureaucratic management. Many of us do not look at company policy as a tool; instead we use it as a weapon to force one and all into total submission. I know some managers more bureaucratic than a chief petty officer. At the slightest challenge, they reach for that policy manual and pull it on you like a gun.

With people mature enough to accept what the rule book says, bureaucratic management works. Others feel totally dehumanized when you drag out a policy-and-procedure book. They feel as if they were being treated as a robot, a mini-computer, a pawn. Also they may decide that you aren't creative enough in your management to adapt to special situations.

Some employees not only want bureaucratic management, they want it in abundance for the satisfaction they curiously receive from regimentation. I know a manager in Washington, D.C., who had two salesmen on his staff who were total opposites. One came from a strong military background and could not understand why the entire company was not standing tall at 7:00 A.M. even though none of the company's clients opened for business until 9:00.

His opposite seldom got moving before 11:30, unless there was a staff meeting to attend or some other function involving his cohorts. For those events, he always appeared promptly. Frequently you might find the late starter at his desk at midnight. He was the second most productive person on the eighteen-person staff, and while his schedule matched no one else's, he never had to ask a secretary to stay late to accommodate his work pattern. He did his work and allowed others to do theirs.

The late starter's unorthodox timetable did not sit well with the early riser, so the latter came to the manager to ask when he planned to put matters in order. The manager got out the company policy manual and showed the dissatisfied party that the rules stated this and the rules stated that; however nowhere did they state a time of arrival or departure for anyone other than the secretarial staff.

The manager acted brilliantly. He didn't shame the early riser into admitting the other guy produced a bit more and caused less hassle for the office staff. Nothing called for that, but the manager did satisfy the man who hungered for bureaucracy when he wanted everyone to toe the line according to the rule book that had become his Bible.

Perhaps this example is not as much one of bureaucratic management as it is an example of doing what works. Management styles have to work, or you haven't managed.

3. DEMOCRATIC MANAGEMENT. We hear this mentioned often today. It does not mean letting everyone vote. When we let the staff vote, when we let the employees make management decisions, that's not democratic management; we are abdicating our responsibilities, and no management takes place at all.

Voting most frequently occurs in small businesses where the person in charge refuses to manage. If one must link democracy with voting power, I can only assume we should find another word to replace the popular term. Democratic management really means letting people participate in the decision-making process.

The vast majority of people maturely recognize that when they do not have the responsibility for the success or failure of an endeavor, they should not have the ultimate authority in making decisions in regard to it. Even though they recognize this, they still feel a need to influence the decision-making process.

Many advantages come from giving people an opportunity to participate in the decision-making process. It gives the manager the opportunity to view events from a number of perspectives, not just his own. In giving these serious audience, any manager should open himself to better decisions.

When a business allows employees to participate in the decision-making process, they feel they are really contributing to the organization and see they are important to the manager. When they receive such respect, they respond tremendously. Some will practically give their lives for the company. But there are the exceptions, like the fellow who, if asked his opinion today, will be in your office tomorrow, when you arrive, sitting behind your desk, with his feet on it.

Nothing works in every case. So we should not view one-to-one management as a frill, a new fangled, mollycoddling gimmick, a trendy caprice of management know-it-alls. No. It is simply the way the most effective managers have worked since free enterprise came along. The big difference lies in the facts that we have gotten around to giving each technique a name and to giving serious thought as to why and when each functions best.

4. IDIOSYNCRATIC MANAGEMENT.   When we use this term for a best management style, we really misname it. We could call all good management idiosyncratic, because all good management is one-to-one and attuned to the individual. When we use the term *idiosyncratic management,* we refer to the extremes of personality, extremes that are literally idiosyncrasies. If we use the idiosyncrasies in developing or working with a person, we have used *idiosyncratic management.*

You probably have someone on your staff who requires an inordinate amount of personal attention. If you go out of your way to provide the "strokes" necessary for him, you practice idiosyncratic management. If you have another who is an egomaniac about recognition, and you go out of your way to find ways to give her recognition, you practice idiosyncratic management. If a third employee likes to be left alone after you set the task and the goal, and you leave him alone—that's idiosyncratic management.

The first manager I ever had mastered idiosyncratic management. He played me like a violin. I was eighteen, holding down my first sales job; and he was eighty-four. The firm sold real estate, and its people were trained to believe they should list a property a day, every day. Now that's unheard of. In fact, no one in the company ever did it for more than brief stretches. Nonetheless, it remained the objective.

On the sixteenth of a particular month, the old gentleman walked over to my desk and whispered, "Stevie, how many listings have you gotten this month?"

I knew he knew. He did not have to embarrass me by asking, but he did. I replied, "Two."

He shook his head and said, "I just don't understand it. I believe I could rent a jackass, put a sign on its back that said BUTLER REALTY COMPANY, LIST YOUR HOME HERE and get a little boy to lead him through the street. If I did, I believe that jackass would get more than two listings in sixteen days."

He knew me. He knew I would have liked to strangle him. He also knew I respected him immensely, and if he could make me angry

Chart 6
Management Review

What weak management techniques have I used?	What were the results?	How can I improve things?
What good management techniques have I used?	What were the results?	How can I use these techniques more effectively?
How have I used the four management styles?	What were the results?	How can I use them more effectively?

enough at anybody or anything, I'd quit sitting in that office, having a pity party, and go to work.

I did precisely that. At six o'clock that afternoon, I drove my car sixty miles an hour through downtown Birmingham to get to the office before he left. When I slapped two listings down on his desk, I said, "Let's see you get a jackass that can get two listings in one day."

"I might," he said. "You'd better get two more tomorrow." And I knew he had me again.

It isn't *what he said* that was good, it was *to whom he said it*. He would never have used the technique on the man whose desk was across from mine. This man, twenty years my senior, would have quit before Mr. Butler could have finished speculating about the productivity of a jackass.

To avoid Fatal Error #5, know your employees as well as you know your family. And do the thing that works to motivate each individual. Use Chart 6 to review techniques you have used and the new ones you have learned.

EVASIVE ACTION PLAN
To Avoid Fatal Error #5 by Learning How to Motivate Each Individual

One of the Fortune Group's tools that has proved successful is "The Fortune Action Contract." After every session, most companies have the students complete it as a means of follow-up.

We have provided you with a contract for use with this program.

Instructions for Completing Action Contract

1. Under 1, write down the single most important idea you've heard during this session.
2. Under "How I will use it," write down:
   A. What you're going to do
   B. When you're going to do it
   C. With whom you're going to do it
3. What will be the benefit for you by using this idea?
4. In our sessions, we give the group a sixty-second preparation break, during which each person enters into a contract with the person next to him, someone else in the meeting, the facilitator of the session, or his manager. We suggest that you choose a person to share with.
   A. Tell that person what you're going to do
   B. Tell him how you're going to do it
   C. Tell him how it will benefit you
5. Make sure you write in the date of commitment and follow-up date for the person you have given this contract.

Fortune Action Contract

Because I feel this is the most important idea for me from this chapter, I make a firm commitment to use it within the next seven days.

1. *This is the single most important idea I got out of this chapter* that I can personally apply:

   _____

   _____

   _____

2. This is how I will use it:

   _____

   _____

   _____

3. What I will gain from its use:

   _____

   _____

   _____

4. Someone to share these ideas with:

   _____

Date of commitment:_____

Follow-up date:_____

FATAL ERROR

6 Forget the Importance of Profit

Earlier I asserted that management has a major purpose: to provide for the continuation of the business. Of course, but in what particular way? The following story holds the answer.

One day the president of a company was having lunch at a downtown restaurant. Halfway through lunch, he realized that four familiar voices came from the next booth. Their discussion was intense enough that he could not resist eavesdropping. He heard each of his managers talking proudly about his department. The chief product engineer said, "It's no contest. The department that makes the most important contribution to the success of a company is the product division. If you don't have a solid product, you have nothing."

The sales manager jumped in. "Wrong! The best product in the world is useless unless you have a dynamic sales effort to get it sold."

The vice-president in charge of corporate and public relations had another opinion. "If you don't have the proper image inside and outside the company, failure is certain. No one buys a product from a company it doesn't trust."

"I think all of you are taking too narrow a point of view," countered the vice-president in charge of human relations. "We all know that the strength of a company lies within its people. Minus strong, personally motivated people, a company grinds to a halt."

Each of the four ambitious young men continued to debate in favor of his area of primary interest. The discussion continued until the president finished lunch. He stopped by the booth on his way out of the restaurant. "Gentlemen," he said, "I couldn't help overhearing your discussion and feel delighted with the pride each of you takes in your department, but I must say that experience has shown me that none of you is correct. No one department of any company is responsible for a company's success. When you get to the heart of the matter, you find that managing a successful company is like being a juggler trying to keep five balls in the air. Four of these balls are white. On one is written PRODUCT. On another it says SALES. The third is labeled CORPORATE AND PUBLIC RELATIONS, and the fourth says PEOPLE. In addition to the four white balls, there's one red one. On it is the word PROFIT. At all times, the juggler must remember: No matter what happens, never drop the red ball!"

He is absolutely right. Without a profit, the company with the finest product, highest image, most dedicated people, and the most impressive financial reserves soon gets in trouble, the kind of trouble that can quickly make a Fortune 500 company only a memory.

The Profit Incentive

Go anywhere in the world and you will find that the paramount way by which anyone evaluates management is its ability to produce a profit. Even if you were in Russia as the manager of a farm or industrial plant, those above you would measure your success by the yardstick of profit—however, they would not describe it with so capitalistic a term. They would call it an "economic efficiency index that determines that amount of surplus left after expenses." In plainer words, they would still judge you on your ability to produce a profit.

You Can't Exist Without Profit

Until the recent resurgence of entrepreneurial studies, I believe that *profit* had become a dirty word, essentially because of the many liberal noncapitalistic notions popular in our society. Quite simply, those who support such ideas have a difficult time relating profit and service. They would give the store away. Primarily because they have lived in a cocoon all of their lives, they have developed a myopic, shortsighted opinion. Those who never shoulder the responsibilities of making the decisions necessary to provide for the continuation of a business or institution miss one of life's great experiences. They have never made a payroll. Until someone has, he or she cannot imagine the true depths of anxiety or total fulfillment of relief. You haven't lived until you've lived through it—it's like white-water rafting.

No business or institution can continue without generating a surplus over and above its cost of operation. Even churches and not-for-profit institutions must maintain this discipline.

One of my close friends, Bill Oliver, resigned his position as vice-president of marketing for a very successful software company, to become the executive director of STRAIGHT, INC. STRAIGHT is a not-for-profit service organization involved in assisting teenagers in dealing with and eliminating drug problems.

Bill and I had dinner to celebrate his first year in his new position. During the course of our conversation, I asked what had been his greatest challenge. He responded, "To get the members of our organization to understand that we cannot help anyone unless we operate our non-profit organization with the same disciplines as any successful business. Steve, we have a great staff of people who have dedicated their lives to helping youngsters with problems. But their service orientation, unless kept in perspective with good business principles, would become their greatest weakness rather than their greatest strength."

Consequently, since its inception, STRAIGHT has refused to accept governmental grants—not for political reasons, but to avoid creating a false sense of security for its management. They operate on the premise that as long as they meet the needs of the community, money will always be available from the private sector. If they manage by the principles Bill Oliver feels are so important, the continuation of the business will occur automatically.

What Contributes to the Bottom Line?

I cannot think of a single managerial position that does not tie into the profit picture of a company. If your one responsibility entails doling out charitable contributions for a large organization, you are still tied in to profit. Of course, the funds you dispense come from profit, but the relationship lies deeper. You act, in effect, as part of the company's public relations activities. If you pour funds into an activity that offends a large block of the company's clients, you will diminish the company's future profits. On the other hand, if your choice of recipients for donations enhances the company's image with the public, you will help build client loyalty and make a contribution toward profit.

Even the managers of the most speculative research and development projects of a company must accept their tie with the profits of a company. While all companies acknowledge that funds invested into research and development are risk capital, none makes investments without the reasonable expectation of discoveries and information that can lead to future profits. It has always been that way.

When Queen Isabella hocked her jewels and footed Columbus's bills, you can bet she wasn't doing it just to prove the earth isn't flat. She expected profitable trade with Cathay.

Accountability Schedule

Few managers see their activities show instant profit or loss. Still, this does not excuse any of us from accountability after some appropriate and predetermined period of time.

In business, investments should always be made with a time factor in mind. If an investment does not show results after a reasonable period, you eat your losses, attempt to learn from your errors, and select another course of action. I have encountered many managers who cannot accept having time limits imposed on themselves, so they shrug off their responsibility to generate a profit. What they fail to see is that they could not be of more service to their enemies if they crossed over the lines and cleaned and loaded the enemies' guns.

Not surprisingly, those quick to dismiss their ties with profit frequently see their budgets trimmed first when times get rough. In other instances a manager who failed to keep his associates properly informed of his department's contributions toward profit will find cuts made in the worst possible places in his budget. The first hit include managers in charge of training, new-product development, advertising, and public and employee relationships. This happens because they fail to make known their direct connection with financial gains.

Faith in Your Convictions

Until the early seventies, Atlanta's transit system was a privately owned and profitable company headed by a master of management, Robert Summerville. Often representatives of other transit systems stood about, eager to learn how anyone could make a transit operation break even—much less profitable.

When the manager of training presented a proposal for a highly sophisticated, new training program to Summerville as a way to reduce the number of accidents and legal settlements any transit operation factors into its annual budget, a chorus of people cried, "Yes, but we have no funds to dedicate to the project."

Summerville responded, "Gentlemen, you seem in agreement that such a program should reduce accidents by ten percent. I want a figure from each of you. If our accidents are reduced ten percent, what would be the savings in each of your areas of responsibility? How much will we save in downtime and repairs on equipment? How much will we extend the life of our vehicles? How much will we save on legal fees, settlements, and the like? How much will be saved on insurance? How much will we improve our enviable public image?"

Once his staff generated the projections, Summerville studied them and said, "Since the cost of establishing this training program is less than ten percent of our legal costs alone, I propose that we show faith

Chart 7
Profit Review

What actions do my people take
on a daily basis?

How do these affect profit?

How can I make management
aware of this?

by transferring funds from legal to training in order to realize an enormous savings. And in case you have forgotten, a penny saved is indeed a penny earned."

The program was installed, was highly successful, and widely imitated. This would not have happened if the training director and his superior had not quite clearly seen the relationship of training to profit.

If you cannot see the relationship between your activities and your company's profits, I suggest that your position is vulnerable at best. Every manager has a responsibility to not drop that all-important red ball.

Using Chart 7, list the ways you and your people directly affect profit. Study them. Impress these links between action and profit upon your people. Help those in management become aware of these connections. The more everyone in a company clearly understands the cause-and-effect relationships between daily activity and the bottom line, the stronger and more efficient your people will become.

Only by constant attention and teaching every one of the people you manage that they contribute can you make sure that the red ball stays up and you avoid Fatal Error #6.

EVASIVE ACTION PLAN
To Avoid Fatal Error #6 by Remembering the Importance of Profit

One of the Fortune Group's tools that has proved successful is "The Fortune Action Contract." After every session, most companies have the students complete it as a means of follow-up.

We have provided you with a contract for use with this program.

Instructions for Completing Action Contract

1. Under 1, write down the single most important idea you've heard during this session.
2. Under "How I will use it," write down:
   A. What you're going to do
   B. When you're going to do it
   C. With whom you're going to do it
3. What will be the benefit for you by using this idea?
4. In our sessions, we give the group a sixty-second preparation break, during which each person enters into a contract with the person next to him, someone else in the meeting, the facilitator of the session, or his manager. We suggest that you choose a person to share with.
   A. Tell that person what you're going to do

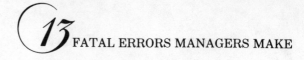

      B. Tell him how you're going to do it

      C. Tell him how it will benefit you

  5. Make sure you write in the date of commitment and follow-up date for the person you have given this contract.

Fortune Action Contract

Because I feel this is the most important idea for me from this chapter, I make a firm commitment to use it within the next seven days.

1. *This is the single most important idea I got out of this chapter* that I can personally apply:

   _____

   _____

   _____

2. This is how I will use it:

   _____

   _____

   _____

3. What I will gain from its use:

   _____

   _____

   _____

4. Someone to share these ideas with:

   _____

Date of commitment: _____

Follow-up date: _____

FATAL ERROR

7

Concentrate on Problems Rather Than Objectives

Oscar B. Ferebee, Jr., president of Goodman Segar and Hogan Residential Sales Corporation, described this Fatal Error to me when he commented, "One reason for the lack of effectiveness on the part of so many managers is that they major on the minors."

When I asked just what he meant, he responded that he had observed that many managers spend as much as 90 percent of their time dealing with problems that only influence 10 percent of their productivity. In many instances, they become so involved with problems that they totally lose sight of their objectives.

Turning Problems Into Opportunities

When I conduct seminars, managers often approach me, seeking a personal conversation. Given a supposedly sympathetic ear, I have found very few talk about their objectives or goals. Almost invariably they concentrate on problems. It's not hard for me to believe then, that what Oscar says is true, but the good manager needs some tools to help him avoid this flaw.

A number of years ago I consulted with a company that recognized this failing of management. In response they attempted to eliminate the word *problem* from the vocabulary of their managers. Their associates referred to *problems* as *opportunities*. I found it fascinating to participate in their staff meetings and hear managers say, "I'm faced with an opportunity I'm having difficulty solving."

They may have changed their vocabulary, but they didn't have tools that eliminate the Fatal Error. One of their managers revealed the futility of this exercise in semantics when he described his attitude in regard to their new marketing approach by quoting Pogo. He said: "Steve, we are surrounded by insurmountable opportunity."

Business Creativity

We call the opposite of concentrating on our problems and losing sight of our objectives "creativity." It fails us when we become absorbed in problems and ignore the end results we wish to obtain. Creativity dies, or at least withers, until we shift our attention back to our objective.

In my opinion, we can best define *creativity* as "the ability to understand the forces impacting upon you, plus being able to use those forces to help you reach your objective." More simply stated, it means "the ability to understand your environment or conditions and use your environment or conditions to your advantage." The very issues and circumstances that first appear as roadblocks to our success can often be used as levers that make success a reality.

First we must stop dissipating our energy by becoming obsessed with our problems and fighting against the situation. Far too many managers act like total nonswimmers. If you put a nonswimmer in a boat, take him out about a mile from shore, and toss him into the water, what will he do? Certainly he will try to swim, but in his panic, he will fight the water. The more he thrashes about, the more he fights the water, the sooner his energy is dissipated, and he drowns. Place a professional swimmer in the same situation, and he will do something quite different. First, he will relax and float or tread water. In treading water, the expert swimmer uses the environment and conditions to sustain himself. Next, he will select a shoreline destination; then at a reasonable pace, keeping the shoreline objective in sight all the while, he will swim to shore. Throughout the entire sequence of events, he uses the water (his environment) as the means to the desired result. Whenever we abandon our objective, we begin to drown, because we have lost our creativity.

Ask a dozen people in management to tell their favorite success story, and almost invariably they describe the use of an obstacle or unfriendly environment as the means to a goal. They may tell you of Volkswagen's move from being snickered at for its homely little bug of a car to an industry giant, simply by making much to-do over the plain but likeable appearance and the easy-to-fix reliability of the product. Others will mention a score of products that have proudly announced that they cost far more than the competition and turned the disadvantage into a sales-winning status symbol: like the haircolor that proclaims that the women who use it are worth it. Many might recall any number of companies that took pride in not being the largest in their industry and equated their smaller size with a wide variety of virtues such as more personal service, quality versus quantity, status, and trying harder.

Our educational system has conditioned us to view as a threat any situation that might disrupt our plans. For the most part, while in school, we were taught that we must have the "right answer," which conditioned us to have a one-answer mentality. That may be true in mathematics; however, in the business world, things are more variable. There is always more than one way "to skin a cat."

When we have set an objective and developed a plan, the factors that may interfere frighten us, because we feel we see the right answer (our plan) destroyed. French philosopher Emile Cartier described the danger in our one-right-answer approach. He said, "Nothing is so dangerous as an idea when you only have one."

Creative managers and those who make the Fatal Error of concentrating on their problems think differently when challenged. Faced with a roadblock to success, the failure-prone manager asks the question "what?" "What will happen to me if I fail?" "What if we don't make our quota?"

The creative manager, on the other hand, asks the question "how?" "How can I use this situation or condition to my advantage?" The very use of the question "how?" presupposes success and that the objective will be reached.

The need for creativity runs through every segment of business. Management is essentially a *thinking,* not a *doing* job. The lifeblood of any organization lies in ideas and creative thinking. The truly successful managers not only learn to view the environment as the vehicle for reaching their goal; they train their people to share this creative perspective. Using Chart 8, convert your problems into objectives and think of several creative ways to reach them.

Atlanta developer Ray Moss faced his most serious business crisis and eliminated a very real threat to the very existence of his business using this brand of creativity.

During the mid-seventies a number of the nation's largest financial institutions found themselves in difficulty. Their situation was created because investments in many REITs (Real Estate Investment Trusts) did not live up to initial expectations. Among these institutions was one of the South's largest banks. Moss had several million dollars in real-estate loans outstanding to them. Due to the pressures, both internal and external, that the bank was under, the financial institution was forced to make a decision not to honor its commitments to many of its

Chart 8
Problems-Objectives Review

Use the chart below to change your *whats* into *hows*, by reviewing your problems and clarifying your real objectives.

Areas I have seen as problems	My real objectives	How the environment can help me	How I can achieve my objectives

customers. Many horror stories can be told by people in real-estate-re-
lated businesses of this institution and others making commitments
one month and the following month saying, "We have changed our
mind. We're calling loans."

Moss found himself in this situation. He and his partners were asked
to attend a meeting at the bank's downtown office, to meet with two senior bank officials who served as troubleshooters in this particular situation. I'll call the bank officers Mr. A and Mr. B. Moss relates that the
meeting began in a very forthright business approach, with Mr. A stat-
ing, "We're going to call the loans."

When Moss responded that they were unable to pay the loans at the
present time, Mr. B became highly emotional, pounded the table, made
several threats, and the meeting quickly deteriorated. Mr. A regained
control of the meeting and said, "Gentlemen, I would like to have you
back here in the morning at nine o'clock to present your plan as to how
the loan will be repaid immediately."

As you can imagine, Moss and his partners, upon leaving the bank,
not only felt upset, they were depressed by the situation. When Ray
Moss arrived home that evening, his daughter, Alyssa, greeted him.

"Come quick, Daddy. Listen! Hear about Br'er Fox and Br'er Rabbit."

Because of his daughter's urging, Moss set his problems aside and
joined her in listening to the audio version of the famous children's
story written by Joel Chandler Harris. His works formed the basis for
the movie *The Song of the South.* Harris built his stories around fanta-
sies about animals and their adventures. In this particular one, Br'er
Fox with the goal of having rabbit stew for dinner, set out to catch
Br'er Rabbit by making a tarbaby, a doll made of tar. His plan was to
entice Br'er Rabbit to get stuck in the tar so that he could capture him.
As Moss listened to the lines of this children's story unfold in song, he
got a creative idea, and he began to understand his environment. A
glimmer of hope appeared when he asked himself how the environment
(the bank's problem) could be used to save his company. He recorded
the tale of the tarbaby on his pocket tape recorder.

The meeting began at the bank the next morning with Mr. B asking
Moss and his partners, "What is your plan for repaying the bank immediately?"

Moss responded, "We have none, because it is an impossibility for
us."

Mr. B once again became very emotional. Moss interrupted the
meeting and said, "Gentlemen, I want you to hear something." He took
out his tape recorder and played the story of the tarbaby. When the
tape ended, the tension was broken, and everyone laughed. Moss
looked the two bank officials straight in the eye and said, "Gentlemen,
the bank is in the tarbaby, too."

After a moment of heavy silence, Mr. A said, "Mr. Moss, I think

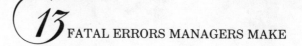

you're exactly right. Perhaps it would be to everyone's advantage to work with you."

Moss's use of the tarbaby story was effective only because it enabled him to capitalize on his environment. Through it he illustrated to the bankers that one more bad real-estate loan would only make their situation worse—not better. The wrapup of the story is that the bank did work with Moss and his partners. Within three years the bank was totally repaid, both principal and interest.

Creating People Problems

Consider your thought pattern when someone under your supervision slacks in production. When a new person whom you are convinced has everything and more that the job requires does not live up to your expectations, what questions do you ask yourself? Do you seek a tangible reason for the lack of performance, or do you ask, "What is wrong with this person?"

If your thought is the latter, you will find a great deal wrong with the individual. When we put anyone we supervise under a microscope and search for faults, we will find them aplenty. This automatically destroys our confidence in the individual and his ability to perform. Unless we are consummate actors (and no manager is), we telegraph our lack of belief in them in a thousand unconscious ways. You can mow down your entire staff with this type of witch hunt.

Managers should never supervise anyone whose success would surprise them. Failure alone should surprise us. When you have determined in your mind that the person is destined to failure, terminate him or transfer him to a position for which he is better suited. Don't keep him around to die a slow death and suffer the agony of being undermined by you.

This faultfinding technique is equally effective in annihilating interpersonal relationships and creating people problems outside the office. If you want to have a perfectly miserable day or evening, you might try this type of thinking on your spouse or a friend. Start now by setting this book aside, and begin to think about the loved one. Every time you think of some quality short of perfection, explore that fault closely before moving on to the next one. If you perform this simple exercise, I can assure you of an evening memorable for its misery. If the other party becomes equally involved in the faultfinding, one of you had better dust off the luggage, because no one building will be large enough for both of you.

The Quest for the Cause

Instead of concentrating on problems by asking yourself what is wrong with the person, consider another option. *What conditions af-*

fect this person's performance? The true cause may shock you, when you see how far it is removed from any personal fault. An illness may have caused it; highway construction may have disrupted business and reduced volume temporarily by diverting traffic; a new competitor may be attempting to buy the market by slashing prices to the bone.

This reminds me of an insurance company that had innovated two types of insurance. For several years, the company offered what seemed the most attractive policies in both areas. Then it happened: Another company introduced a combination of the two policies, because most of the prospects who needed one of the policies needed the other as well. Sales of the combination policy were brisk. Management of the innovating company raged at its sales force for not trying hard enough. Still sales continued to sag. Finally management became so exhausted from its emotional outbursts that it quieted down enough to hear the suggestion of an agent who had hung on during the storm. His suggestion was so simple it took time to sink in. He pointed out that management was quite right in saying that the combination of their two policies gave superior coverage to the competition's single umbrella policy; so why not combine their two policies into one, pass the administrative savings along to the customers, and continue to offer the best coverage at a reduced cost?

I am embarrassed for the company to report that management pondered this simple, creative advice for a full year before combining their policies and beginning the uphill climb to reestablish itself in an insurance field that it had created.

What's your goal as a manager? If you keep your sights on it, not on the pitfalls, pratfalls, and problems between you and it, you will avoid Fatal Error #7.

EVASIVE ACTION PLAN
To Avoid Fatal Error #7 by Focusing on Objectives, Not Problems

One of the Fortune Group's tools that has proved successful is "The Fortune Action Contract." After every session, most companies have the students complete it as a means of follow-up.

We have provided you with a contract for use with this program.

Instructions for Completing Action Contract

1. Under 1, write down the single most important idea you've heard during this session.
2. Under "How I will use it," write down:
   A. What you're going to do
   B. When you're going to do it
   C. With whom you're going to do it

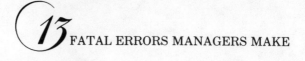

3. What will be the benefit for you by using this idea?
4. In our sessions, we give the group a sixty-second preparation break, during which each person enters into a contract with the person next to him, someone else in the meeting, the facilitator of the session, or his manager. We suggest that you choose a person to share with.
   A. Tell that person what you're going to do
   B. Tell him how you're going to do it
   C. Tell him how it will benefit you
5. Make sure you write in the date of commitment and follow-up date for the person you have given this contract.

Fortune Action Contract

Because I feel this is the most important idea for me from this chapter, I make a firm commitment to use it within the next seven days.

1. *This is the single most important idea I got out of this chapter* that I can personally apply:

   _____

   _____

   _____

2. This is how I will use it:

   _____

   _____

   _____

3. What I will gain from its use:

   _____

   _____

   _____

4. Someone to share these ideas with:

   _____

Date of commitment: _____

Follow-up date: _____

FATAL
ERROR
8   Be a Buddy, Not a Boss

So often managers want to be the employees' buddy after hours, then come into the office and manage them tomorrow—and the employees will not allow it. It is an either-or situation: You must be the buddy *or* the manager. Successful hybrids do not exist in such a situation.

Most managers have received advice through the years concerning how they should conduct themselves when in the company of those they manage. I believe that most of the advice is an expression of the personal convictions or mores of those passing on the advice.

For example, a few years ago, I attended a full-day management seminar with different instructors in the morning and afternoon sessions. The question of management behavior with the employees was brought up in both sessions. The morning instructor responded by recommending to the group of seasoned managers in attendance, "Never, under any circumstances, have a drink of alcohol with the people you manage." I thought about this at lunch and decided, based on the man's recommendation, that he probably had never had a drink in his life.

The afternoon instructor, in response to the same question, recommended, "Whenever you can, have a few drinks with your people. It relaxes everyone." I surmised that he must be a drunk. Neither instructor's advice gave a firm principle for conduct that can be used in many situations.

I suggest a broader guide. At the very least in your employee-manager relations: *Never do anything with an employee that you would not do with your firm's number-one client or customer.* If you have a policy of not drinking with your best customer, do not think that you will be able to do so with your employee. Whatever might offend your client might offend the person who works for you, and it is your responsibility to treat him as of the same worth as the person who makes your business possible by paying for your goods or services.

Concerning the question of drinking, many corporations now have rules that require complete abstinence of their staff. But to others this question will become a problem. I know that in the "real world" people do drink, and I'm not qualified to be a rehabilitator. But it only seems in a manager's best interest for him to be circumspect in this area. Drinking may well be bad for your business. Drunk managers are bad managers, and drunk salesmen are bad salesmen.

Simply, if we're not circumspect in our actions with our employees it is because we do not respect them. If we fail to respect them, they certainly will not and cannot respect us. Remember this: When a manager is in the company of an employee, it is never entirely social. The company picnic or Christmas party may be social for the employee, but for you it must be business. This doesn't mean you shouldn't relax, enjoy yourself, and have a good time—just as long as you remember that while you are with the people you manage, the situation is a professional, business relationship.

Management Trouble Spots

Managing Former Peers

In my experience the managers who have the greatest problem with wanting to be the buddy and the boss came up through the ranks to a position that requires them to supervise people with whom they used to share equal rank. The combination of a manager-employee relationship with old friends often becomes a high, difficult-to-clear hurdle.

Higher management may lessen the new manager's temptation to try playing the dual roles of buddy and boss by remaining sensitive to the situation and placing him over people in an office removed from his former one. Since this is not always possible, often the new manager must work out a solution. Too often, the following happens. The new manager wiggles out of social invitations with a string of flimsy excuses. The old buddy gets his feelings hurt, decides the manager has become full of himself, starts an office-sized cold war, and everyone involved suffers.

Instead a man who handled this very well indeed sat down with each of his old pals individually and told them, "Remember those talks we had about what a good manager should or shouldn't do? Well, when I heard I was up for this position, I wrote down every point I could remember, and that list is on my desk. I've made myself a promise to reread it at least once a week. Since our relationship has changed, I hope it'll be a change for the better for both of us. As your manager, I want to give you the support you need. In return I want you to give me the performance I need. Neither of us admires managers who try to be a chum at lunch and a slavedriver the rest of the day. I won't follow that pattern either. I want ours to be the best possible *professional* relationship, and it'll take work on both our parts to make it the best. Let's go for it. Okay?"

With that, he extended his hand, and without exception, his former pals extended theirs in relief and gratitude for the fair managerial stance the new manager proposed.

But what happens to the manager who tries to act like a buddy on and off the job? The answer is he doesn't manage. There may exist some variation of committee management, but most often, no management takes place at all. Soon at least one employee figures out that the nonmanaging pal is being paid a manager's salary while not doing the work. Then a breakdown process begins.

Being a Family, Not a Business

Some small companies get through a few years of buddy-buddy nonmanagement. Then the company grows a little, and the new employees arrive but have no place to turn for clear managerial direction. Everyone tells the new arrivals what to do. If the person who should have been managing all along finally sits down in the driver's seat, everyone rebels, because everyone feels demoted.

Too many small companies try to function as a family, not a business. When they grow, they lack the foundation for organized expansion. In these cases, a series of painful, unnecessary, and costly reorganizations have to be endured by all, from the people supplying capital to the person on the bottom rung of the company's ladder.

Soul Mates

Some managers make an even greater mistake and get swept up in the situation of trying to be the lover and the boss.

That's wrong. It's unethical. It's an abuse of power. If none of those high thoughts interest you, maybe a little note about self-preservation will.

Not long ago, I sat and listened to one married manager confide how wonderful it was to have a soul mate for a secretary. Oh, it was togetherness all the way. But love is definitely blind (and so is lust); therefore the manager failed to see the reactions of the other employees. Soon a higher level of management noticed the negative effect, and the manager's job flew out the window with the speed of one of Cupid's arrows.

Even an honest romance between two single people is not the best relationship on the job. If a manager falls in love with an employee, it doesn't mean that the romance shouldn't blossom, but it certainly should bloom in a different hothouse. The manager should get the employee transferred as quickly as possible, preferably, before the first date—even before the first furtive glances are exchanged. While a different department will do, a position in a noncompetitive company is the better choice.

Why? Because a manager has control over the rewards given to the people under him. So there must be no doubt about his ability to deal rationally and without favorites.

Not Limiting Your Responsibilities

No matter how fiercely independent any of us are, we all want friends and all need a few close ones. Sometimes we must work hard to resist the temptation to seek out those friendships with those we manage. After all, we spend the bulk of our waking hours at our jobs. Still, we need to avoid such situations, because of the problems close friendships at work can create.

A manager should never step into the trap of playing the role of parent, priest, pal, or psychiatrist. These roles belong to others. The manager's responsibility is to be the manager in an employee's life—nothing more.

Many managers don't have time left for managing after they have finished the list of extraneous tasks they assign themselves. No manager should assume the responsibility of operating a human relations agency for its own sake. The manager's job description does not include social work that will make everyone feel loved, protected, and adored.

A manager should never become more concerned about his or her people's success or failure than they are; the responsibility for their success or failure lies with them, not with the manager. Learn this lesson: *You cannot be responsible* for *people; however, by necessity, you must be responsible* to *people.*

When managers become responsible *for* people, we overstep our managerial boundaries and adopt those individuals. This was perhaps the single most difficult management lesson for me to learn personally. I finally got it through my head through an experience I had several years ago.

Our firm employed a salesperson whom I managed directly. He had been reasonably successful. Suddenly his production took a nosedive. He no longer produced at the minimum levels required by our company. I discussed the situation with him and informed him that production must increase. To assist him, in accordance with our company policies, he was placed in our personal improvement program for re-training. Still no results. Company policy was clear. The man should be terminated, and I had the responsibility to do so. I could not bring myself to do it. He had seven children. I knew that the economic opportunities for him in our organization were greater than that available anywhere else, because of his age and the economy. Whenever I thought of his termination, I thought of the children and backed off.

Finally, I made a trip in his territory to conduct a seminar. He approached me at the first break and said, "Steve, I've got something to tell you!" and requested I meet with him after class.

Man, did I get excited! Do you know what I thought? What I believed he was going to do? Quit! Do my job for me.

We got together for lunch immediately after the session, and I could hardly wait for him to tender his resignation. Throughout the meal he totally avoided the issue. In near desperation over our third cup of coffee, I said, "You said you had something to tell me. What is it?"

He responded, "Steve, it's so difficult."

Probing for the resignation, I told him, "You can tell me anything, brother."

With that, he sheepishly said, "Steve, I've fallen in love. I'm leaving my wife and kids!"

At that moment I recognized that I felt more concern for his children than their father did. They were *his* responsibility, not mine. I failed this man miserably. I failed my company, and I failed his wife and children when I attempted to become responsible *for* him. I was reparenting a fifty-five-year-old man. I had refused to treat him as an adult. Had I been responsible *to* him rather than *for* him, if I had respected him enough to treat him as an adult . . . when he failed to do his job with our company, if I had done mine—terminated him and let him handle his responsibility of supporting his seven children, he would not have had time to fall in love.

Parents who effectively manage children use "tough love." When you are a manager in the business arena you just call it "honest management." Adopting our employees makes it practically impossible to practice honest management. Our adoption causes us, in many instances, to fail them by cutting corners or covering for them. In others it causes us to decide we're going to force them to succeed, whether or not they want to. It is impossible to force growth. These attempts to shoulder responsibility for people form the single greatest cause of wasted time and money and management frustration. I've known of managers who couldn't sleep, who woke at 2:00 A.M. and paced the floor, worrying about the success or failure of an employee. But most often the employee lay comfortably asleep in his bed. You cannot help those who will not help themselves. No person worthy of his or her job wants to be adopted. Instead valuable people seek to be treated as ma-

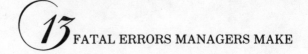

ture adults. Management is true reality therapy. You allow people to contribute like adults, or you allow them to leave.

Hard Decisions

No one ever said management was easy. If it were, then anyone could do it, and management would not receive wages in excess of those paid the employees. Managing can often become a painful experience, and you may incur pain while developing the mental toughness required by the job. Managers not only have to make tough decisions regarding employees, the toughest decisions affect their personal discipline and sometimes their families. In the life of every manager there comes a day when he or she cannot play the clown.

One Friday night I came off the jet way and out into the concourse at Hartsfield International in Atlanta. I saw a neighbor of mine, waved at him across the way, and he waved back. As I began to walk on, I saw that he looked miserable. He didn't look as if he had strength enough to get to the baggage-claim area. I walked over, took his briefcase in my hand, and walked with him. "George, where have you been?" I asked.

"I've been to Boston."

"What were you doing there?"

He said, "Steve, I don't know what you know about the road construction business, but we've been through hell on earth. I thought our company was going under several times in the past two years. The contract I secured today saved us. The pressure is off. We've got it made."

I thought his reaction was one of those anticlimactic responses where you build yourselves up and then experience a letdown. I said, "George, why are you so low? I would think you'd be so excited you'd be hitting the ground about once every ten feet. Are you ill?"

He shook his head and said, "No, Steve, I'm not sick, but I've never been so miserable in my life. I did not get to play the clown."

Then he related his story. "When I left home about seven this morning, I told my wife, 'Honey, you can count on me. I'll be home this afternoon at four-thirty. Now I know I've promised I'd be here before and have been late—but not today. I remember being late to the dinner party on our anniversary, but you can count on me. I'll be home today by four-thirty.' "

That afternoon at 5:00 their little daughter was having her fifth birthday party. For two weeks she had been going throughout the neighborhood telling all the kids, "Oh, come to my birthday party. It's going to be so neat. Come and meet the most wonderful, funniest clown in the world. My daddy's going to play clown!"

Arriving at his office, George received a phone call. They had the contract. However, it was an international situation, and the only time they could have all parties together was that day. If he wanted the business, he needed to be in Boston that afternoon. George flew to Boston. That night when he went home from the airport with that contract in his briefcase, it wasn't like the movies. He didn't go home to find some tall, willowy blond in a flowing negligee. He didn't go home to candlelight or roses or champagne. He went home to find a woman who was upstairs, exhausted from holding a birthday party for twenty kids and trying to explain all afternoon long to a five-year-old why her daddy wasn't there to play clown. *This is the personal discipline required to manage.* Please don't misunderstand me. George loves his family as much as any of us love ours. If he hadn't cared, he wouldn't have hurt.

He went to Boston in spite of the hurt, because in addition to his own family, he was also responsible *to* 200 other families. There is a rule that we have to live by to manage and manage effectively. It doesn't sound very nice, but it sums it all up: *To manage you cannot put the welfare of any individual above the welfare of the organization.* Everyone who manages effectively lives by this rule, and sometimes it hurts.

A World War II incident involving Winston Churchill illustrates the point perfectly. The British had broken one of the Germans' secret codes and were privy to information coming right out of Hitler's high command headquarters. From the decoded messages, Churchill recognized that the Germans planned to bomb Coventry, England.

He had a choice. He could evacuate Coventry and in doing so jeopardize the integrity of the secret, thus hurt the war effort. On the other hand, he could maintain the integrity of that secret, allow the Germans to bomb Coventry, and risk the lives of thousands of men, women, and children.

Winston Churchill let the Germans bomb Coventry.

I thank God that none of us in management will ever make a decision where thousands of lives hang in the balance, but we *will* make decisions that are, for us, just as difficult emotionally. Our ability to manage will increase in direct proportion to our ability to make the emotionally difficult decisions.

What difficult management decisions are you avoiding? List them in Chart 9. Study them and admit to yourself the consequences of continuing to avoid living up to your title of manager.

EVASIVE ACTION PLAN
To Avoid Fatal Error #8 by Being a Boss, Not a Buddy

One of the Fortune Group's tools that has proved successful is "The Fortune Action Contract." After every session, most companies have the students complete it as a means of follow-up.

We have provided you with a contract for use with this program.

Chart 9
Management Trouble Spots Review

Tough people decisions I'm avoiding	Course of action

Instructions for Completing Action Contract

1. Under 1, write down the single most important idea you've heard during this session.
2. Under "How I will use it," write down:
   A. What you're going to do
   B. When you're going to do it
   C. With whom you're going to do it
3. What will be the benefit for you by using this idea?
4. In our sessions, we give the group a sixty-second preparation break, during which each person enters into a contract with the person next to him, someone else in the meeting, the facilitator of the session, or his manager. We suggest that you choose a person to share with.
   A. Tell that person what you're going to do
   B. Tell him how you're going to do it
   C. Tell him how it will benefit you
5. Make sure you write in the date of commitment and follow-up date for the person you have given this contract.

Fortune Action Contract

Because I feel this is the most important idea for me from this chapter, I make a firm commitment to use it within the next seven days.

1. *This is the single most important idea I got out of this chapter* that I can personally apply:

   _____

   _____

   _____

2. This is how I will use it:

   _____

   _____

   _____

3. What I will gain from its use:

_____

_____

_____

4. Someone to share these ideas with:

_____

Date of commitment: _____

Follow-up date: _____

FATAL ERROR

9

Fail to Set Standards

The concept of setting standards is not a favorite of many managers. In fact they'd probably like to avoid the subject altogether, because they view standards as a means of making up punitive rules used to punish those who fail to produce or who avoid conformity.

Those with such a negative definition of that word misunderstand one of the keys to a well-run company. For the guidelines a company makes need not aim at forcing compliance to a list of regulations, but should have the goal of building personal and corporate pride.

The Importance of Standards

Everyone has standards, as shown by this story I read in an article by *Atlanta Constitution* staff writer Jim Auchmutey.

Rick and Cherokee are the envy of their peers. They make decent money, wear designer clothes, and own more watches than a jewelry store.

They largely associate with their fellow "canners," a shadow population of professional scroungers whose survival depends on collecting aluminum cans. The $150 to $200 a week the two young men earn by dredging dumpsters may seem modest, but affords them luxurious lifestyles by the standards of their fellows, most of whom are alcoholics and homeless.

Rick and Cherokee are lucky. They live under a bridge. From the dumpsters behind bars and apartment complexes along their middle-class canning route, they acquired furnishings for their place and salvaged their designer wear.

"Some people think we'll just crawl right into a dumpster," says Rick, who wears a Sasson shirt and a BORN TO LOSE tattoo. "That ain't so. I look it over, and if I see maggots—even if the dumpster's full of cans—I don't want it. *I got standards.*"

Regardless of our economic or social strata, we all use certain principles that separate us from the "also rans" and boost personal pride. Whether these are written in a corporate manual, described in an organization's literature, spoken of frequently, or never consciously dealt with at all, they do exist in such areas as morality, ethics, dress, and performance.

Ask not, "Will standards be set?" But, "Who will set the standards?" In a business situation, the well-run company will have policies outlined by management, for if their leaders decline to do so, the employees will take the initiative, and the results may be less than pleasing.

No Nudity

Every company recognizes a bottom line as to what they will tolerate from their employees with respect to any standard. The higher our expectations in this regard, the greater the pride in working with us. Our ability to retain valuable people increases in direct proportion to our expectations; if they cannot have pride in their association with the members of our organization, good people will not derive self-esteem and will not affiliate with us over a long period of time.

Several years ago, while on vacation, I lost my way. In search of reliable directions, I stepped inside a small storefront real-estate office. At the third desk back sat a man with his feet propped up on the desk. He wore no shoes. Not only that, he wasn't wearing trousers, but sported ragged, cut-off jeans and a faded T-shirt that touted a rock group. His uncombed hair, three-day growth of beard, and the unmistakable smell of bourbon that encircled him hardly appealed to me. However it would be unfair of me to say that this office had no dress code. I am certain they did not allow nudity. If he had shown up naked, they would have sent him home. You could not allow some character to remain on your staff and dress this way. If you did, you would lose your good people. They would refuse to associate with such riffraff.

While I didn't inquire, I'm certain that this unkempt individual was equally as well informed about the company's ethical, moral, and production standards. I'd guess that they were on a par with the dress code. But, however low, standards did exist.

When Standards Are Respected

Properly presented, standards tell employees exactly what calibre people they associate with. Comfort and assurance can result from positively presented standards. They can form a source of pride in the organization just as long as the stated standard matches the real one revealed by management decisions.

A few years ago I worked with a firm that had a minimum dollar-volume production standard for its people. I saw one man resign because he knew he wasn't going to reach the standard, while another made a personal purchase of $11,000 to meet the $600,000 minimum. Certainly no doubt lingered in the minds of this company's employees as to its standards.

A friend's son, Kelly, told me that he planned to resign from one insurance company and go to work for another. I knew from talking with Kelly's father that the young man had not been making his quota. Assuming that Kelly had opted for resignation instead of being fired, I asked, "Well, do you think this new company's products are so far superior that they will be easier to sell?"

Kelly's reply surprised and pleased me. "Not at all," he said. "It's a matter of standards, performance standards. I knew that if I didn't make my quota at the old company, it didn't really matter, because they just keep on giving you another chance. With this new company, it's a different story. You produce, or you go, and I need that sort of discipline. At my age I've got to be surrounded by winners. I find it too easy to listen to the losers."

Apparently that was exactly what Kelly needed, because the next year he almost made the Million Dollar Roundtable. He had a clearer understanding of the importance of this firm's quality standards than his first employer did. Kelly drew pride from the higher standards and the personal test they gave him.

Standards have the desired effect only when management practices what it preaches. We cannot say one thing and do another. As in the firm Kelly was associated with, announced standards not adhered to become pride destroyers rather than builders.

I learned recently of a printing company where the workers rebelled because management rehired a man after he had been fired for smoking marijuana on the job. The workers took the position that the man knew the rules, had broken a trust, and could have endangered his fellow workers by mishandling the machinery. In the employees' view, he did not deserve a second chance. The standards of this printing firm were precious to the workers. They would not let them slide.

Now, I am not naive enough to believe that all the workers who clamored for the man to be fired never broke the rules. But clearly, they did not choose to allow anyone to endanger others by violating an ethical and safety standard. I believe the same would have happened if the man had deserted his post while running a press. When there exists a practical reason for any standard and that reason is communicated to the people, they will respect and uphold it.

Each time a manager feels tempted to bend the rules, he must realize that he will not actually bend the rule, but he will make a new one. If he gives the employee caught with his hand in the till a second chance, this creates a new rule: It is okay to get caught once. No matter how quiet the manager tries to keep his decision, the word gets out and spreads. The employees either rebel, as in the case of the printing firm, or they acknowledge it as a lowering of standards. While they may not assume that just anyone can get away with, say, stealing, they clearly understand that a new rule has been set up for the manager's pets. Rules that do not apply to all shatter pride.

Performance Standards

Certainly one may more easily track performance levels in some jobs than in others. For instance, the productivity of a salesperson may show more clearly than that of a person affiliated with a nonprofit or service organization. Nonetheless, there always exists some means by which management may gauge significant service or productivity, some system recognized and understood by both the manager and the employee.

For example, how do you measure the production of a research scientist under your supervision? If he calls you into the lab to show you he has actually found the cure for the common cold, that's production. If he calls you into the lab to show you he has stumbled on something in his cold cure research that has an effect on weight control, that's progress. But what if he only can show that twenty experiments tried had no effect on the common cold? Is that progress? Yes. And it is measurable progress. You now know that twenty more roads are dead ends. You have narrowed the possibilities. The man's work is measurable, therefore a production standard can and should be set before you assign the scientist to a lab.

A manager-scientist at Bell Labs once identified the key role in his management as helping the scientist in his area select doable projects. Even in pure science there is an art of management.

I believe that if a manager cannot devise a means by which he and his employees can measure production, that very little management takes place. The measurement must be realistic, fair, and must have an ultimate link with keeping the red ball—profit—afloat.

The research scientist in a pharmaceutical company's lab may seem far removed from the company's profit margin, but he has just as much impact on it as the salesperson. We do not place the scientist in the lab to keep him out of the rain. He is there for a purpose. The company invests money into his work in anticipation of a marketable discovery.

If you don't think so, ask an AT&T executive why they kept Bell Labs. Ask them whether or not the invention of the transistor or fiber optics contributed to the bottom line.

Thomas Edison, the creator of the research-lab concept, never forgot that research was fed by funds from profit, and profit came from research. He went so far as to set a *weekly* quota on the number of inventions he wanted to present to the patent office.

Essentially we may track performance in four major areas. One or more of these will fit any job classification:

> Quantity
> Quality
> Timeliness
> Cost

QUANTITY.   Our most common method of measuring performance depends in some fashion upon quantity. In one way or another we tally number of sales made, dollar-volume generated, number of hours billed, number of fenders painted, or any amount that may be processed or produced.

QUALITY.   Here is one of the most important areas for which standards apply. Measurements from the quality standpoint include at least two factors: errors and appearance.

Errors can include monitoring rejects, misfiles, safety records, customer complaints, miswelds, and countless other areas.

Appearance deals with items other than rejects or specific errors and is more subjective in judgment. It covers such areas as neatness, a person's manner in answering the telephone, a receptionist's greeting of visitors, or a service representative's explanation to a dissatisfied customer.

TIMELINESS.   More often than not, our third method encompasses responsibilities such as meeting deadlines for on-time shipments, on-time departures and arrivals, or absenteeism. Timeliness also can involve new and workable approaches. The most creative idea needs the right moment for its introduction.

COST.   Most often we relate cost to the basic three *m*s of Management: men, money, and materials. Is the person able to perform, while controlling the capital expenditure for labor, management time, materials, and corporate services? Can he live within the budget?

Standards in Decision Making

In addition to increasing employee pride, standards may serve as a great asset in eliminating management pressures. Properly utilized, they remove the personality from our tough decisions. Guidelines established by objectively examining what management should reasonably expect an employee to do as a minimum provide a basis for businesslike decision making.

For instance, imagine you're the manager of a firm of CPAs. Your firm has established a minimum standard that each junior accountant bill not less than 2,000 hours per year, or 450 hours per quarter. Once you have properly communicated this standard, it provides the basis for counseling the employee without personality becoming involved. The employee who fails to achieve knows he has not kept pace. Should you decide to terminate the individual, the reason for the termination is clearly business.

A manager must know when he has done his job in order to survive. Standards have enabled me to maintain my managerial equilibrium over the years. The most severe threat to that equilibrium occurred several years ago. A man I managed was not making minimum standards. After numerous counseling sessions and an attempt to retrain him with no results, I fulfilled my management responsibility by terminating him. At the close of our last interview, he shook my hand and said, "Steve, I will never forget you or the company. You have put forth more effort to help me succeed than I could have expected. I'm not quite sure why I didn't make it, but I know the fault is mine, since so many others not only make the minimum, but go far beyond it." He left my office at 2:30 in the afternoon. At 5:45 I was called back from the parking lot with an emergency phone call. My former employee had died of a heart attack at 4:30. When I heard of his death, I became physically ill at the thought that my actions had caused it. The sleepless night that followed was one of the worst in my life as I wrestled with the thought that I had caused the man's death. I nearly closed the doors of my business, but surely that would have been unfair to the others who depended upon me.

At last I realized that death was in God's hands, not mine. I could only console myself with the knowledge that I had done all I could to keep him in the job and help him perform. I began to understand how a surgeon feels when he has done his best to heal a patient's body, but the patient dies. The only comfort he may have is that he has done his job.

My company's standards enabled me to look his widow in the eye and serve as pallbearer at his funeral, because I knew I had done all I could do. I had been fully responsible to him.

The Covenant

We need to view standards as a covenant between a company and its employees. Various kinds of union and employee contracts exist. But

Chart 10
Standards Evaluation

Areas in which standards should be set	Methods to set them
	Quantity
	Quality
	Timeliness
	Cost
	Quantity
	Quality
	Timeliness
	Cost
	Quantity
	Quality
	Timeliness
	Cost

contract, in the old sense of the word, meant an agreement based on understanding, good faith, and mutual commitment; today we would probably call it a covenant. A covenant goes one step better than our present understanding of a contract. The company guarantees the employee that by its upholding of the standards, the employee will enjoy a certain quality of work environment and career opportunities. In turn, the worker will uphold the standards in order to enjoy the benefits those standards assure.

The wise company takes its policy manual to its public-relations consultant and asks that the wording be examined carefully. Are the standards expressed in positive terms? Is the benefit of each standard spelled out? Is the wording clear and easily read? The answer to each of these questions must be a solid yes!

When all involved view standards as a covenant, a pledge of quality, pride in the company grows stronger and stronger—and management becomes easier and easier.

It's easy to avoid Fatal Error # 9, if you set and clearly communicate reasonable, honest, mutually agreed upon standards for your employees and see that everyone—including you—abides by them. Use Chart 10 to develop your guidelines.

EVASIVE ACTION PLAN
To Avoid Fatal Error #9 by Setting Standards

One of the Fortune Group's tools that has proved successful is "The Fortune Action Contract." After every session, most companies have the students complete it as a means of follow-up.

We have provided you with a contract for use with this program.

Instructions for Completing Action Contract

1. Under 1, write down the single most important idea you've heard during this session.
2. Under "How I will use it," write down:
   A. What you're going to do
   B. When you're going to do it
   C. With whom you're going to do it
3. What will be the benefit for you by using this idea?
4. In our sessions, we give the group a sixty-second preparation break, during which each person enters into a contract with the person next to him, someone else in the meeting, the facilitator of the session, or his manager. We suggest that you choose a person to share with.

FAIL TO SET STANDARDS

    A. Tell that person what you're going to do
    B. Tell him how you're going to do it
    C. Tell him how it will benefit you
5. Make sure you write in the date of commitment and follow-up date for the person you have given this contract.

Fortune Action Contract

Because I feel this is the most important idea for me from this chapter, I make a firm commitment to use it within the next seven days.

1. *This is the single most important idea I got out of this chapter* that I can personally apply:

_____

_____

_____

2. This is how I will use it:

_____

_____

_____

3. What I will gain from its use:

_____

_____

_____

4. Someone to share these ideas with:

_____

Date of commitment: _____

Follow-up date: _____

FATAL ERROR

10

Fail to Train Your People

In previous chapters I attempted to establish the principles for influencing the performance levels of our people. In Fatal Error #1 we defined *management* as "the skill of attaining predetermined objectives with and through the voluntary cooperation and effort of other people." In Fatal Error #2 we stated management's major purpose is to provide for the continuation of the business in our absence. In Fatal Error #3 we mentioned that the difference between the successful person and the nonsuccessful person is that the successful individual has developed the habit of doing the things unsuccessful people do not do. In Fatal Error #9 we pointed out the importance of standards to both our people and management, that performance could be measured from a standpoint of quality, quantity, timeliness, and cost. At the risk of simplifying the complexity of management, our job might best be described as *inducing our people to behave properly,* that is, getting them to consistently perform at a level of *PAR* (*PAR* meaning performance at or above our minimum standards). A manager's job can, in many respects, be summed up in the form of two essential challenges:

> Getting people from entry level to *PAR* performance
> Maintaining *PAR* performance once it's attained

PAR Performance

Only the unwise manager will try to separate an employee's actions or performance from those influences coming before them (we call these precedents) or the consequences that follow them (we call these results). Instead he will want to use these to help maintain and increase productivity in those for whom he is responsible.

PRECEDENTS.   These come before action, serve as guides or standards in evaluating future behavior, and form the foundation of performance. Examples include job descriptions, training, policies, objectives, or other people's actions.

ACTION (OR PERFORMANCE).   This is what employees say or do. We see it in activities of the job, such as typing a letter, making a sales presentation, giving an injection, cashing a check, or operating machinery.

RESULTS.   These are the consequences of the action, which cause the employee to repeat, modify, or in some cases discontinue the action. Recognition, a compliment from the boss, increased pay all serve as meaningful results. Negative ones, which cause people to modify or discontinue action, include ridicule from co-workers, lost sales, customer complaints, and reprimands.

Together these elements determine the behavior of our employees. Precedents trigger action. Action produces results. And results determine future behavior. (*See* Illustration 4.) *P*recedents, *a*ction, and *re*sults equal *PAR*.

Illustration 4
PAR Formula

PRECEDENTS ➡ ACTION ➡
RESULTS ➡ FUTURE BEHAVIOR

Manager's Obligations

Several years ago, the governor of a state having turmoil in its prison system was asked what its administration planned to do about it. The governor replied, "We're never going to have better prisons until we get a better class of prisoners." Sharing that attitude, many managers often view the failings of an employee as the employee's problem, rather than a management weakness.

Certainly we make mistakes in staff selection. On occasion managers find themselves trying to fit a square peg in a round hole, but such cases are the exception, rather than the rule.

If the hiring manager has not made a mistake in selection, only three

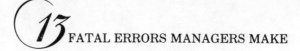

basic reasons remain for why a person does not do his or her job. These apply to you, to me, to everyone under our supervision.

1. The individual does not know what the job is
2. The individual does not know how to do the job
3. Someone or something interferes with his or her desire or ability to do the job

These three reasons for nonperformance constitute our basic obligations to our people. We have not begun to be responsible to them until we have assumed the responsibility for establishing the basic precedents to successful behavior by making sure they know what the job is and how to do it. Nor have we begun to lead until we have strengthened our people so that they might withstand the conditions and the people who would interfere with their desire and ability.

Clarify the Job

When observing the employees of a company that has brought us in to consult with them about increasing productivity, I frequently feel as if the employees are crying out to management, saying, "I'll dig your ditch: Just tell me how wide, how deep, how long, and in what direction." Until they know, they cannot perform. Management must provide this direction.

My next statement may not sound very nice, but it is true: All new people are incompetent.

I don't care who you hire or what his background or track record shows. I don't care if she went to Harvard Business School or learned everything they don't teach you there. Even if he was the prize employee of a competitor, when he joins your company, he remains incompetent until he knows your policies, procedures, filing systems, and so on. If newcomers have never worked in your particular business arena, they are really incompetent.

Your competitor's secretary, top salesman, best mechanic, or most productive researcher may prove useless to you, because what constitutes a valuable employee in your company is nothing more than *a person who will do what you want done.*

Every time I hear a manager relate problems with new employees who balk at certain responsibilities, I remember that truth. Then I ask, "When you interviewed this person for the job, did you present a job description that included this duty?" Usually, I am told no written job description existed, that the task may have been overlooked in the verbal rundown—*but* everyone who ever held the position always did the task, because it came with the territory.

The manager assumes a certain job title means exactly what he wants it to mean, while the prospective employee assumes a different list of responsibilities. In effect, they sign different contracts when they agree to work with each other.

I hear other managers complain about the performance of a person promoted from within. "John knew what the job involved when I gave it to him. He's had the desk next to Sam for two years, and I certainly expect him to do all the tasks Sam did."

John may have been too busy doing his old job well to take copious notes on Sam's activities. At some point, preferably the starting point, the manager should have given John a complete list of responsibilities.

While I don't recommend the by-the-book approach as a means of settling every single argument concerning who makes the coffee, who answers the phone when the receptionist momentarily leaves the front desk, or who refills the copy machine with paper, I do feel that a written job description makes two important contributions to the smooth running of your department:

> It tells the employee exactly what you expect of him or her
> It tells you exactly what you expect of the employee

If you study that list of responsibilities carefully, you may learn why the last secretary always ran into overtime; you may see that the job requires much more detail than you ever realized; or you may unearth a score of other issues that either need serious discussion during the interview phase or reworking on your part. In any case, it will clarify, in your mind, what you truly expect of an individual in a particular position.

You may realize that you are not clear as to what the person should be doing or how to best utilize his talents. If you have not or cannot list all a job entails, do not feel surprised when the employee leaves work unfinished.

Today, employees are particularly sensitive about the unglamorous facets of business and react strongly when they learn you expect them to do unpleasant or menial chores such as call late payers, refile papers someone else removed from the files, or serve coffee to a client. While no job includes only glamorous tasks, employees do deserve to know what ration of unglamorous work comes with the title, and they should know before accepting a position.

If you are thinking, *Yeah, well, I don't have time to sit down and write out detailed job descriptions; I'm too busy trying to manage this place,* let me suggest that a large portion of your management hassle would vanish if people clearly understood their responsibilities. I suggest that if there were a job description for your title (and there should be), near the top of the list should be "Develop job descriptions and review them with each employee."

Expect Action, Not Thought

I make this recommendation: When you bring a new person onto your staff, do not expect him to *think;* employ him to *do; you do his thinking for him.* By doing so, you teach him how you think. When he learns your approaches, when he learns how you think, he has taken the first step toward becoming a good employee, that is, a person who will do what you want him to do. To expect the new employee to solve the riddles of your business puts him in a position of attempting to give you answers when he doesn't even know your questions. You must understand that your organization is a whole new world for him. Without past experience to rely on, he has no point of reference for decision making. Consequently, the odds are at least fifty-fifty that any decisions he makes will seem poor ones. I read of one, perhaps extreme, example of decision making with an improper point of reference that illustrates the point perfectly.

A missionary in the Chad region of Africa dealt with a very primitive group of people who had only worked in metals for two years. Each day, the missionary noticed, her houseboy took an empty tin can with him. When she asked him why, he proudly responded that he was planting the tin cans in order to grow an automobile.

To us this may sound ridiculous, but consider the houseboy's agricultural point of reference. His experience had taught him if you want something, you plant a seed and grow it.

Some managers rebel at my recommendation that they think for their employees initially, because they view this recommendation as a put-down of the employee. Certainly that was not my intention. It has nothing to do with the employee's intelligence. Thinking for the employee when he first joins you not only provides direction, it gives the new hire an opportunity to feel like a winner. By doing this, you help him immediately become a team player. New employees left to their own devices experience a lot of unnecessary stress in becoming part of the new environment. They feel like orphans.

Each new hire, on a daily basis preferably (and in no case less than three times a week), should meet with his or her manager or supervisor. In case of a detached employee, hold these meetings by phone.

The first day's meeting should establish precedents by providing the employee with a list of each activity he needs to engage in that day. Discuss the activity, to ascertain your employee's understanding of how you want it handled. Subsequent meetings serve two purposes: to establish additional precedents and to review the results of the previous day. This affords an immediate opportunity to recognize and reinforce the desired behavior, and while the new employee is learning exactly what you want, you're discovering his strong points and weaknesses. These day-to-day meetings should take place for the first three weeks of the new employee's tenure.

A word of caution: At least two things are imperative. When taking this approach to making sure people understand the job, you must follow up and be practical in your recommendations. If you establish a precedent with an employee by giving direction and telling him you will check back with him, failure to do so defeats your entire purpose. In effect, it teaches the employee not to follow through. You may have experienced this lack of followup during your days as a student. Did you ever have a teacher give you a difficult homework assignment and fail to collect the work? Assuming you did the homework, you felt cheated. In fact, you *were* cheated, and you had something far more valuable than money stolen from you—lack of followup robbed you of both your recognition for accomplishment and a sense of success. If the teacher did this more than twice, you quit doing the homework. The same rule works in business.

Keep your recommendations practical. The indoctrination of a new employee should not become a form of hazing. Outside the military, it is not boot camp. Through it, you only need to direct new employees into productive activities.

The worst example I've ever seen of impractical recommendations involved a twenty-one-year-old real-estate salesperson named Bobby Hite. When we first met, he was a student in a sales training course I was conducting. In his eagerness to succeed he would practically tear the information from you. In each of the first three sessions he sat in the front row, his eyes ablaze with excitement. At session four he attended class in body but not in spirit. My concern caused me to seek him out after class and inquire what troubled him. He informed me he planned to drop out of sales, because he could not cope with the frustration of talking to 100 people a day. I found this almost unbelievable and asked that he share his call records with me. We met for breakfast the next morning, and he showed me the names of over 3,500 people he had talked to in the past seven weeks.

Bobby informed me that the salespeople with his company had heard an audiotape by a man who attributed his success to distributing 100 business cards a day. Bobby's manager supposed that if 100 business cards were good, 100 contacts would be better. I had Bobby accompany me while I met with his manager, who was a personal friend. After discussing the futility of the 100-calls-a-day approach, we agreed that Bobby would follow the regimen of helping two people a day; that is, engaging two people in meaningful discussion about listing or purchasing real estate. After 100 calls a day, this was a snap. Within two years, Bobby became one of the leading salespeople in Nashville, Tennessee. The last time I saw Bobby was at the National Association of REALTORS® Convention in New Orleans. He proudly showed me his 1099 form. He had earned a six-figure income the previous year. Imagine, all of that talent could have been wasted, literally burned out by impractical activity.

How to Do the Job

After making sure our employee knows what the job is and the activities in which he must engage in order to accomplish it, the next logical step in attaining *PAR* performance is training. Regardless of what we expect, a person's performance level directly reflects his skills. Unfortunately, many of us in management ignore our training obligation. This occurs for four essential reasons:

1. We assume that people possess the skills when they join us, since they have often occupied a similar position with other companies, been in another department with our firm, or have good educational credentials. We take their ability to perform for granted.

   I've heard many managers sound the death knell for increased performance by saying, "We don't need to train. We employ only experienced individuals." Situations change, procedures and technology change and yesterday's skills cannot sufficiently meet today's challenges.

2. No one trained the manager. He rose through the ranks on talent and personal discipline. He prides himself on being a self-made individual. Such naturally gifted people find it frustrating to watch novices struggle with a task that now seems second nature to them. Regardless of the job title, there's no such thing as a "natural."

   Years ago, I heard Zig Ziglar say he had read a lot of birth announcements. They always indicated that the newborn was either a boy or a girl. He had never read of the arrival of a doctor, salesperson, accountant, or member of any other profession. Performers in any field are developed, not born. However, some individuals do possess much more God-given ability than others. Some athletes possess more natural ability, some people have more natural musical talent than others, and the same truth applies to any field. A few individuals who have never taken a music lesson and who can't read a note sit down at the piano, run their fingers over the keys, and play a tune. When I was a boy, they called this "playing by ear." Many managers perform the tasks their people face just as naturally. They do it by ear. Unfortunately, performing any job in this manner shares this aspect of playing the piano by ear: You either can or cannot do it; and if you can, you can't transfer that ability. The one who does this has a special gift. We cannot solely staff our organization with the gifted. There just aren't that many special people available. We, like the music teacher, must find people with enough sensitivity to music that they can hear the sound and read the notes. Then we must encourage them to practice until they become proficient.

3. We don't understand what's required to modify behavior and develop skills. My closest personal friend, Fred Miller, is in the insurance business in Birmingham, Alabama. I never quite understood why, but for a number of years Fred experienced a sizeable turnover in clerical positions in his small company. I was most impressed with one of his new employees. At the first opportunity I complimented Fred on her. His response was that he planned to terminate her. Shocked, I asked, "Why?"

He said, "She's stupid!"

I told him I thought she was super. How could he feel that way?

Part of her job, he replied, was to do mathematical calculations. She was doing them by hand, while a calculator sat idle on her desk.

I said, "Fred, she doesn't know how to use the calculator."

He snapped, "She does!"

"She can't!"

"She *does* know how to use the calculator."

"How do you know?"

Indignantly he responded, "I spent ten minutes training her."

Obviously, Fred did not have an understanding of what it requires to develop such a skill or the patience to train.

4. In large companies where training departments exist, managers often feel that the responsibility for training lies with the training department, not with them. They fail to understand that a training department acts as nothing more than a support system for management. Managers and supervisors cannot spend their time with people who do not have the capacity to produce. Training departments develop new hires from entry level incompetence to a stage of maturity that justifies management time. Some managers destroy this most valuable asset when they tell the new hire who has just completed basic training, "We do it differently in the field." Training departments cannot provide the line manager with a finished product. Attaining and maintaining *PAR* performance require both basic training (which normally occurs in the classroom) and coaching (field training).

Education and Training

First, understand the difference between training and education. Failure to do so prevents many managers from assisting their people in skills development.

Providing knowledge is the purpose of education. When you evaluate an educational program, you consider what a person has learned by the end of a course. On the other hand, training does not provide knowledge, but uses it as a tool. A training program aims at action, and you evaluate it by what people can and will do. Training must be more highly organized than education, because the result of disorganized knowledge is confusion. Confused people will not take action, so a training program that does not clarify defeats itself.

Have you ever heard the old saying, "Those who can, do, and those who can't, teach"? I'm in the teaching business, and I've heard it often. I must admit that most of my life I've considered it an insult. With maturity, I came to realize the truth of this statement. In many instances those who teach cannot perform, because skill level does not increase in direct proportion to what we know. Even if your entire staff is composed of walking, talking encyclopedias who seem to know all about your business or their job, they do not really possess skills until they can get the knowledge from their minds into action. We define *skill* as "the ability to readily and easily utilize knowledge, in order to perform."

Most of my adult life, I've been in the skills-building business. Even though I intellectually understood skills, I did not have a gut-level realization of their importance until a few years ago.

I have avidly hunted throughout my life. I grew up in Alabama, hunting with my father, who gave me my first firearm, a Stevens double-barrel 410-gauge shotgun, for my tenth birthday.

Four years ago, the week before Thanksgiving I gave this same gun to the son of a friend of mine for his tenth birthday. Since the youngster, Robert Soto, knew he would get the gun, I promised to take him on his first dove shoot. The minute Robert got the gun, he was ready to leave for the hunt. I refused and said, "Rob, if you own a gun, you must know how to handle it properly. Firearms are dangerous; occasionally they will go off unexpectedly."

We went into the backyard and, without shells, went through the motions of loading the gun and pulling up on the stock to close the breech—never pulling up on the barrel. "Keep that barrel pointed at the ground and pull up on the stock—*always* the stock." The boy didn't enjoy the drill any more than I did at his age, but he went through it in order to get to go hunting.

Later that day, we drove up to the dove field where ten or twelve other hunters had assembled. As we got out of the car some birds flew over. Two men shot, each hitting a bird. With this, I reached into the car trunk, removed a double-barrel 12-gauge shotgun, broke the breech, placed two shells into the chamber, and closed it. The gun went off with a deafening explosion. In gut-wrenching horror, I saw a man twenty feet away get hit in the back, from his head to his buttocks. His voice rose in horror, "I'm hit." Grasping the back of his head, he started to run.

My friends and I stopped him. We pulled his jacket and shirt up, his pants and underwear down, and saw not a mark on him, not a scratch. I looked back and realized with relief I had shot into the ground. What had hit him had been the ricochets—the dirt and perhaps some pebbles. The only one reason I did not kill that man—if not kill, at least severely injure him—is that when I was ten, my father trained me to always close the breech of a gun by pulling up on the stock, never the barrel. If I had closed the breech that day by lifting the barrel and leveling the gun, I could have cut that man in half. Now, let me assure you, thirty years after being trained by my father, when I closed the breech, I did not think *stock*. It happened instinctively. I had developed a skill.

The point I'm attempting to make is that until people can utilize knowledge readily and easily as an instinctive reaction, they have not been trained. They do not possess skills.

Classroom Training

Whenever possible, conduct the initial aspects of training in a group. Economically this makes much more sense. If you put ten people in the group, you have one hour of instructor (management time) for ten hours of training. In many instances the very fact that a group exists insures that the training will occur. Where one individual is to be trained, the manager often overlooks him to deal with some perceived crisis. A group environment also allows trainee feedback. They can gauge their progress in comparison with that of others.

A training session begins in the mind of the instructor. This should start with a one-sentence statement of purpose involving the action desired. If the statement of purpose requires a half page or paragraph, the success of the training becomes doubtful. If the instructor cannot state the purpose in a clear, concise manner, it probably means he is confused, and the class will be in even worse shape. When you work with a group throughout a day, you may need a number of one-sentence purposes; but remember, you can only accomplish one at a time.

After studying the classroom training formulas of hundreds of trainers, we recommend one: the *uncover, discover, recover* formula. It establishes three purposes in training people to take action.

UNCOVER.   This step tells us that we must uncover a need for this material within the mind of the student. People will absorb only the bare minimum of information necessary for them to reach their goals or objectives. If the student's mind is not open, if he cannot relate to a personal need for the material to be covered, he receives very little from the training experience. Every training class begins with three types of participants: those who are there to learn, some who are on vacation, and in most instances a few prisoners. The instructor successful in uncovering can create learners.

DISCOVER.   In the second phase of training, you teach the knowledge necessary to perform the skills. If the instructor effectively uncovered, this really turns into a discovery, an *aha!* experience for the student. Teaching methods over recent years have become rather sophisticated; however, "show and tell" still works best. People learn most rapidly when presented with explanation and demonstration.

RECOVER.   Most trainers fail here, where we move from education to training. Recovery is designed to provide the students with hands-on experience. It provides maximum student participation. The most common methods used include drills, role play, and case studies. The recovery phase affords students a platform for their fledgling attempts to perform.

Provide the right atmosphere. Many trainers, in an attempt to recover, defeat their own purposes. Student participation requires *good* finding, never faultfinding. *Do not punish the learner.* Trainers often fall into the trap of recovering to make sure the person has it right. Recovery needs to provide feedback so that the students know what they know.

Ignore mistakes and praise progress. Initially, progress is what we're seeking. Perfection comes a step at a time. Training in a good-finding environment seems almost contrary to human nature, which tells us if you want to help a person improve, concentrate on removing his weaknesses. This approach leads us to offer negative critique. Countless trainers have approached the learner with machete in hand, chopped out the weaknesses, and then watched the person bleed to death in perfection. Progress and behavioral change come through increasing strengths. The weaknesses then fade from the picture. The training arena has no place for ridicule, sarcasm, or negative critique. It demands an environment in which initial failure is acceptable. Anything worth doing is worth doing miserably for a while. Make your training program a confidence-building process. When you ignore mistakes and praise progress, you build confidence.

Several years ago I read of an experiment conducted at a major university to demonstrate the effects of good-finding as opposed to faultfinding atmospheres in training. A class in report writing for junior executives was taught to two groups by the same professor. In both, he taught principles, and the students were given the assignment of writing reports. Classes then critiqued reports. The professor allowed only positive criticism in one of the classes. In the first class, where there were no restrictions on the critique, the students received more feedback on their mistakes than their successes. Where only positive critiques were allowed, they heard only praise for their progress. When the classes concluded at the end of a month, those who had heard about their mistakes felt more inhibited and less effective than when they began. Those who heard only about their successes increased their ability many times over.

At times you feel there must be some reference made to mistakes. If this is the case, ask each student, "If you had it to do over again, what would you do differently?" If the material was presented properly in the discovery phase, each will tell you every mistake he made. When people point out their own errors, you avoid a faultfinding environment. The ego of the learner can accept self-criticism; criticism from others is at worst ridicule and at best a reprimand. Remember: Never punish a learner. Reprimand only when desired behavior has been previously demonstrated.

Coaching (Field Training)

Once we provide the basic or classroom training, we have just begun. Regardless of the business or industry, we must make continuous coaching or field training a fact of life for the manager/supervisor. A friend relates that one of his senior instructors in medical school greeted the new class by saying, "I'm going to spend one month teaching you how to do abdominal surgery—and three and a half years teaching you what to do if something goes wrong."

Give the word *field* a broad interpretation. Coaching takes place on the job: The field for the receptionist means the reception area; for the mechanic, the garage; for the accountant, the client's books; for the salesperson, the customer's office; for the nurse's aide, the hospital floor. The field is wherever the person works.

We as managers face the essential challenges of getting the person from entry level to *PAR* performance and maintaining it. The word *PAR*, which represents the three elements of influencing behavior—precedents, actions, and results—provides us with a simple yet truly effective coaching model or procedure. Let's relate this to coaching.

> P—PRECEDENTS—*those things that serve as a guide and standard for future action.*
> The most effective precedent when coaching is "show and tell." The coach should let the student observe the job being

done, then explain how it was accomplished. Then he needs to ask the trainee questions to make sure he understands the procedures. If necessary, the sequence should be repeated until the trainee understands the procedure.

A—ACTION—*what an employee says or does.*

Give the trainee an opportunity to attempt to perform the task while being observed. The procedures of showing and telling constitute only education until the employee has a hands-on experience.

R—RESULTS—*the consequences of the action.*

Positive reinforcement, including compliments and recognition of achievement, cause people to repeat the action. In coaching, as in classroom training, *never* punish the learner. Reinforce the desired behavior by praising him on his progress. The process is then repeated until the employee attains acceptable levels of performance.

Positive reinforcement of the desired behavior forms effective coaching. But most trainers find that time consuming. We live in a "quick fix" society. Unfortunately, no quick fixes work in increasing productivity. The desire for an instantaneous solution pressures us into faultfinding. Helping people to develop skills requires knowledge, understanding, and patience.

When I was a boy, we owned a pet chicken. My father trained him to come out of his roost, go into another cage, and peck on a trigger to get corn. I'll bet you know how he did it. Sure, he put down a trail of corn to the trigger. After a period of time the chicken knew to go to the trigger in order to be fed. The bird received positive reinforcement by being fed along the way.

We do exactly the opposite in business. The quick-fix manager, rather than putting out a trail of corn, prefers to put an electric shock in the sides of the cage. If we punish our learner, an employee, or a chicken by giving him electric shocks through negative feedback, he withdraws. The negative reinforcement inhibits the learner and causes him to retreat from action.

Interference with Desire and Ability

Earlier I stated that the third reason people do not perform is because someone or something interferes with their desire or ability to do their jobs. Some of the occurrences that interfere lie beyond your control: serious illness, marital problems, death of a close relative.

Five groups of people may destroy a person's desire to produce: coworkers, relatives, friends, customers, and managers. Let's take on these villains one at a time.

CO-WORKERS.   His new staff mates can make life miserable for the new person, especially if nasty little cliques form within the work force. To eliminate hazing, try assigning each new person to a seasoned employee who takes on responsibility for helping the newcomer with orientation problems such as locating forms, learning names and titles, and becoming familiar with procedures.

Unwisely some managers make the same person responsible for orienting every newcomer, forming a new power clique. And whenever possible, have someone of comparable rank responsible for the newcomer.

FRIENDS.   Those with whom he has close relationships can also become villains who undermine the new person's desire to perform. It is no help at all to have a new employee's friend say, "Aw, come on. You can play tennis today," or to say to the person with a briefcase of materials that need a full night's study, "You're crazy to drag work home from the office, especially when I'm standing here with two tickets to tonight's game."

You cannot round up employees' friends and stop them from undermining the new person's drive. But you can strengthen the newcomer's defenses. I know one manager who tells each new employee, "You and I both know that it is going to take extra concentration the first few months on this job. We know it, but your friends may tend to forget. I guarantee you that one or more will try to talk you out of doing your best."

He then challenges the person to make a game of guessing how many times it will happen within a certain amount of time. Turning serious temptation into a challenge to say no takes much of the pain out of turning one's back on pleasure. The individual also becomes aware of his or her inner strength.

CUSTOMERS AND CLIENTS.   For those in a sales or service capacity, customers and clients may undermine a person's desire and ability to perform by destroying belief in the company and its products. People who have customer contact, either in initiating business or in servicing clients, will by necessity deal with people who reject them in some fashion. For the salesperson initiating business, the prospective customer may compare your product unfavorably with those of competitors. The person in a service capacity will be called on to smooth the feathers of dissatisfied individuals. If this occurs before the employee experiences a deeply rooted belief system in your company, his desire may diminish.

FAMILY.   The next block of troublemakers may wait for the person at home. A young man looks over the opportunities available and selects a career in selling. Excited about the opportunity and its potential, he runs home to share the good news with the most important person in his life: "Look, Mom, I'm going into a commission-with-base situation that can net me thirty thousand dollars a year!" She responds: "Darling, you'd better get a real job."

Family members often believe a degree should guarantee an executive position. To the offspring excited about the possibilities for advancement from an entry-level position, Dad observes: "Yes, but what guarantee do you have that you won't be stuck in this flunky position forever?"

I saw an example of this situation when a friend of mine, who had been a star quarterback on his high school football team remarked to his son, who was playing guard, "Why aren't you in the backfield? That's where the glory is!" The son, who didn't possess his father's athletic ability, quit the squad within two weeks.

A married woman entering business may begin with a husband who may be thrilled over the prospects of the additional income. When her success outstrips his, he may feel a threat to his manhood and begin to force her out of her career.

You will have few opportunities to deal directly with the family. Most of the contact comes through the employee. But in many cases, you can arm your employee with written as well as verbal information that combats family doubts. By your acknowledging that family members do worry, the employee will find it easier to talk with you about pressures and will present you with the opportunity to provide supportive counseling.

With the spouse who may feel threatened or neglected, the best approach is to draw that husband or wife into the employee's success. Take any opportunity to thank him or her for being supportive of the employee. The sooner this is done, the better. Don't wait for signs of trouble to prompt you to speak up. The old axiom "An ounce of prevention is worth a pound of cure" never held more truth than in this type of situation.

THE MANAGER. This book is all about this greatest of villains. When we fall prey to any of the 13 Fatal Errors, we lessen the desire and ability of those we manage. Be on your guard—do not fail to train your people. Use Chart 11 to review your situation.

EVASIVE ACTION PLAN
To Avoid Fatal Error #10 by Training Your Staff

One of the Fortune Group's tools that has proved successful is "The Fortune Action Contract." After every session, most companies have the students complete it as a means of follow-up.

We have provided you with a contract for use with this program.

Chart 11
Training Review

In what areas do my new employees need to be brought to *PAR* performance?	How can I help?

In what areas do my old employees need to be helped to maintain *PAR* performance?	How can I help?

Instructions for Completing Action Contract

1. Under 1, write down the single most important idea you've heard during this session.
2. Under "How I will use it," write down:
   A. What you're going to do
   B. When you're going to do it
   C. With whom you're going to do it
3. What will be the benefit for you by using this idea?
4. In our sessions, we give the group a sixty-second preparation break, during which each person enters into a contract with the person next to him, someone else in the meeting, the facilitator of the session, or his manager. We suggest that you choose a person to share with.
   A. Tell that person what you're going to do
   B. Tell him how you're going to do it
   C. Tell him how it will benefit you
5. Make sure you write in the date of commitment and follow-up date for the person you have given this contract.

Fortune Action Contract

Because I feel this is the most important idea for me from this chapter, I make a firm commitment to use it within the next seven days.

1. *This is the single most important idea I got out of this chapter* that I can personally apply:

   _____

   _____

   _____

2. This is how I will use it:

   _____

   _____

   _____

3. What I will gain from its use:

_____

_____

_____

4. Someone to share these ideas with:

_____

Date of commitment: _____

Follow-up date: _____

FATAL
ERROR
11
Condone Incompetence

In Fatal Error #10 we reduced the complexity of management to two major challenges: getting people from entry level to *PAR* in performance and maintaining acceptable performance once it is attained.

In the process of training people I urged you to avoid punishing the learner. I suggested that you never reprimand a person until he has demonstrated the desired behavior. When you look at the characteristics of the really successful manager, without exception, you will find: *Successful managers refuse to condone incompetence.*

Avoid Condoning Incompetence

How easily we condone a job inadequately done, if we become careless and follow the easy path. As managers we fall into this trap for several reasons:

> Because we feel the need to be loved and seek it in the office
> Because we hope the problem will disappear if we ignore it
> Because we lack the willingness or ability to confront others

THE NEED TO BE LOVED. We all need to feel loved. Certainly no one is so staunchly independent that he does not want to have others like him, but managers must settle for respect in the workplace. The one who absolutely must be loved will never perform his job effectively.

Stop and think about the people you have worked for. See if you can isolate the one who seemed to you the most effective manager. Now rate that person on a 1-to-10 scale, with 1 being easy, and 10 being firm.

Several studies show that most people give their best managers about a 7.9 rating and explain that these managers were both firm and fair. From the combination of firmness and fairness came the respect shown by employees.

When a manager allows the need for love to override his responsibilities, he becomes a pushover who allows unacceptable behavior and accepts any excuse for nonperformance. He does this because he fears being branded a taskmaster. Believe me, some in the work force can spot a love-starved patsy of a manager and land a position under that person's supervision in an amazingly short time. Other employees, who would not normally seek out such a situation, find it hard to resist the temptation set squarely before them. Seek love outside the office; respect must remain the goal of the successful manager. Don't let management become a popularity contest.

THE DISAPPEARING-PROBLEM ACT. In other instances we simply hope the problem will go away. We see the deviations in behavior necessary to maintain *PAR* performance as momentary lapses in concentration or minor inconveniences.

AVOIDING CONFRONTATION. Our third reason for ignoring incompetence results from our never having developed the ability or willingness to confront. This problem is partly one of conditioning; all of us have experienced confrontation in the past. We have memories tucked away of parents, teachers, ineffective managers, or others who confronted us, but their actions didn't help. Instead of causing us to improve our behavior, we continued the pattern, with the additions of resentment, anger, and bitterness.

Those parent, teacher, or boss confrontations proved counterproductive because those in authority did not handle them properly. Confronting incompetence requires skill and timeliness. Each time we ignore a deviation from acceptable behavior, it has a tendency to become greater. Eventually, the gap grows so wide we can no longer ignore it and are forced to confront. By this time the deviation has become a major irritant. We become emotionally involved, often angry. *Never confront in anger.* When riled, we have a tendency to attack the individual rather than confine our discussion to job-related behavior.

Here is what happens. A manager expects an employee on the road to call the office each Monday, Wednesday, and Friday. The individual misses a Wednesday call, but the manager doesn't mention the incident when they talk on Friday. Then two weeks later, he misses a Monday call. The next week, he misses both Monday and Wednesday. When he does call on Friday, the manager greets him with, "You've been on vacation, buster? Exactly where were you?" It is over! The manager lost all chance of productive communication.

Another manager allows his receptionist's lunch hour to expand, day by day, to an hour and twenty minutes. Suddenly he explodes, "Where did you get the idea this is a part-time job?" Again no productive communication will occur.

A third manager waits for a subordinate's weekly reports. After a month of waiting, he scalds her with his words, "Have you no sense of responsibility?" Once more, it is over.

Positive confrontation calls for the manager to act quickly, before the problem grows. The first time you spot a deviation that could grow into a serious issue, don't take time to jot it down on your "to do" list. *Confront immediately.*

Punishment Is Not the Purpose

If you do not wish to antagonize your employees (and what purpose would that serve?) do not make confrontation a means of punishment or take this action simply to decrease the deviation. Using a broader view, you will want to encompass increasing the desired behavior, which will be of benefit to both you and your staff member. If you use the following techniques, you will be able to correct employees, not punish them.

NEVER CONFRONT IN ANGER. We have seen already the damage this can cause in the workplace. When the manager displays such emotion, it tends to trigger the same reaction from the employee. Under these conditions, he will not hear what the manager says, because he is too busy defending himself. When a leader so loses his self-control, others begin to lose respect for him. Soon he gains a reputation for moodiness, and his employees see that as the basis of the confrontation, rather than any actions on their part.

CONFRONT IMMEDIATELY. By putting it off, you risk making the situation much worse. Instead, before the deviation repeats itself, talk to your staff member and iron out the problem. You will find this much easier than trying to solve a larger problem later.

Grievance procedures, company, government, and industry regulations may influence the timeliness and methods for dealing with unwanted behavior, and the rules of your ballgame may differ from those in other businesses. Use these as required, confronting as early as possible within the stated limitations.

CONFRONT PRIVATELY. *Never* reprimand an employee in public. Mistakenly believing that if they correct one in front of a group, they will not have to reprimand all, some managers have tried this tactic. And it backfires terribly.

When a staff member receives such a reprimand, the peer group perceives not an attack on the individual, but one on the group. Even those who have not previously identified with the individual rally around him, because human nature causes others to defend the underdog. Now the manager finds himself in the unenviable position of being the enemy of all.

Give some consideration to the placement and timing of the reprimand. In addition to making certain it is done privately, see that no one else even knows it has taken place. Do not conduct all such confrontations in your office, and avoid closing the door only when reprimanding, or you will invariably be signaling that someone has been called on the carpet.

"See me" notes should not precede reprimands or, for that matter, any conversation with an employee. Even when you do not plan to reprimand, such messages alarm people. First they wonder, *What did I do wrong?* and the resulting apprehension reduces communication drastically.

BE SPECIFIC. When confronting an individual, pinpoint the unwanted behavior, rather than defeating your purpose by attacking the individual. For instance, you might say, "Your report was a day late," instead of, "You're wasting time." People can relate to and will change actions, but they cannot do that with broad accusation. Ambiguous indictments dealing with attitude, personality, and intelligence cause resentment.

USE DATA. By supporting your statements with specific facts, you'll put the numbers to work for you. This information should be readily available if you have been measuring performance from the standpoint of quantity, quality, timeliness, and cost. Employees who have received this data all along already know where they stand, so make it available to them. When you share the facts, you may more easily focus on performance as opposed to personality. Use this important tool in building a case for improvement, and you will avoid dismissals.

BE CLEAR. When you deliver a reprimand, make certain the employee knows that is what you have done. Let him know how you feel, share your concerns and frustrations, and tell why this behavior creates these emotions. But under no circumstances deliver a compliment and a reprimand simultaneously. Attempting to ease the pain of the reprimand with a compliment creates confusion. For instance, if you say, "Last week your customer contacts were down 20 percent. You need to make more calls. I know that you can do it, because you're a good worker," the salesperson may remain uncertain as to your meaning. He may even feel he has been complimented on his work habits.

PROVIDE REDIRECTION.   If you mention the undesired behavior and do not redirect your employee by reinforcing the action you want, you've missed the purpose of the reprimand. Now you have merely punished the employee without correcting his actions. Specifically mention the behavior you seek, making certain the employee *thoroughly* understands what you desire. Get a definite commitment from him, which should encompass not only what he will do, but the time frame in which the correction will appear.

FOLLOW UP.   Make an end to the confrontation, and do not bring it up again, except by reinforcing the desired behavior. Constantly reminding the employee of his failings will not serve your purpose now. Instead you catch your worker doing something right and make him feel good about his accomplishments.

How to Confront

Effective confrontation is a skill. You may only develop skills when you clearly understand a procedure that works. No one set of words will suit every situation, and you will want to vary them for each individual, but some techniques can prove helpful to you. Guided by the ones I have outlined here, you may plan the confrontation, observing the principles we have just established. Through use and practice of the following steps, you may perfect confrontation into a skill.

> WHAT   Point out the specific behavior you have observed.
> HOW   Tell him how it makes you feel.
> WHY   Let him know why you feel that way. Relate to the employee's needs, objectives, sense of pride. Avoid your own needs.

These first three steps pinpoint and emphasize the unwanted behavior. The subsequent steps, represented by the word *GAP,* serve to redirect their actions.

> G—GET HIS OPINION. Make sure that the employee understands the importance of the situation.
> A—AGREE ON WHAT WILL BE DONE. Redirect him to desired behavior. Establish the time period in which the correction will be made.
> P—POSITIVELY REINFORCE THE DESIRED BEHAVIOR. Recognize him for his accomplishment, in public if possible.

By way of example, you notice that your customer-service representative, Jeanne, is late for work. Now is the time for one-to-one management. Call her aside. Simply state *what* you have observed.

"Jeanne, I noticed you were twenty minutes late this morning. "

She knows she was late; now she knows you know. You made a straightforward observation of behavior. Next tell Jeanne how this makes you feel: frustrated, confused, concerned, or merely curious. The reaction that practically everyone accepts is your being frightened.

"Jeanne, I noticed you were twenty minutes late this morning. *Your tardiness frightens me because. . . ."*

The next step is to let Jeanne know *why* you feel the way you do.

"Jeanne, I noticed you were twenty minutes late this morning. It frightens me because *our customer service desk was not staffed. Our company's entire reputation has been built on quality service. Any reduction in that service is unfair to those who have confidence in us and to every member of our team."*

Said with sincerity, the above works. On the other hand, try, "I saw you arrive late, and it made me mad! I'm paying you to be here." This will not work, because it focuses only on your wants and needs. No matter how loyal an employee is, she is not likely to slit her wrists for the company. There must be personal focus on the one being managed. Once you've told her what behavior is undesirable, how it makes you feel and why, you have pinpointed and emphasized the incompetence. This should be followed with the *GAP* procedure.

Get her opinion: "Jeanne, do you understand my concern?"

Some instances—depending upon the situation—require discussion before the person relates to the severity of the situation.

Agree on what will be done. In this instance, if Jeanne's delay was caused by a delay in traffic, it might entail getting her to leave home by no later than 7:05 A.M.

Positively reinforce. Follow through by observing Jeanne's arrival time. Catch her doing something right and recognize her. Praise her for her progress.

Use Chart 12 to identify persons on your staff whom you need to confront. The *GAP* techniques you have learned here will help you effectively rectify the situation.

Spotting the Early Signs of Sag

Several examples in this chapter deal with being tardy. I used these for several reasons, not the least of which is that they exist in every work environment. They also provide us with a simple method for demonstrating the technique. More important, repeated tardiness or absence is usually the first symptom of greater problems.

Some companies have voluntary meetings before or after regular work hours. For years I have held a weekly voluntary meeting with my sales force on Saturday mornings. While not required, the attendance gives me an excellent barometer. Those who start missing the meetings

Chart 12
Confrontation Guide

Behavior I need to confront	What I've observed	How it makes me feel	Why I feel that way	Desired behavior change

or fail to touch base via long distance always soon start showing sagging production.

If you see sag in production, it probably means you missed correcting a sag on behavior.

Another manager I know uses the device of asking his people to jot down a list of issues they would like covered at staff meetings and submit them on the day preceding the meeting. Those who stop having issues they feel need covering soon show some form of poor performance.

These early signals of trouble give the alert manager the opportunity to start looking for the cause of the problem and to deal positively with it before symptoms become evident to the entire staff.

Using Positive Reinforcement

The *PAR* formula for increasing productivity taught us that when results are meaningful to employees, they continue action. Meaningful results most often take the form of recognition and praise. But how many of us effectively praise our employees? We have trouble being complimentary, and when we do try it, often we praise or compliment the individual personally. If we wish to achieve results with this formula, we should compliment specific behavior.

I felt so sorry for a manager who led me around a convention to meet his company's top performers. His best efforts at positively reinforcing his people seemed pathetic. He would say, "Steve, I want you to meet Dot, one of our superstars." Or, "I want you to meet Bill. Wow, he's a real pro!"

He meant well, but how does the salesperson repeat being a "superstar" or a "real pro?"

If the manager had pointed out some specific behavior, some actions that made them a superstar or real pro, each would have had something they could repeat or improve.

Like confronting, positive reinforcing is a skill, and in order to perfect it, we need a technique. Try the *what, how,* and *why* approach previously recommended.

Consider the reaction of Dot if her manager had introduced her in this way. "Steve, I want you to meet Dot. She's on the phone for a minimum of one hour three nights a week, canvassing. Every time I see her there I become even more proud of her, because I know that even though she's already our number-two performer, she'll double her income through this activity." With the *what, how* and *why* approach he would have spotlighted an activity she could repeat and perhaps even improve.

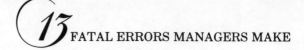

When the Procedure Fails

I would like to be able to guarantee that these procedures will work in every case, but if I did, I would be lying. Some people will not respond. It is then time to ponder the question *Have I failed, or have they?* The questions in Chart 13 should give you the answer.

Chart 13
Negative-Performance Review

	YES	NO
1. Did I make certain that he knew what the job entailed?	__	__
2. When he started, did I give him a tracking system?	__	__
3. Did I make certain he knew the activities to be performed?	__	__
4. Did I do my dead-level best to train him to do all that I expected of him?	__	__
5. Did I give him standards, so that he could be proud of associating with the organization?	__	__
6. Have I avoided creating sag situations myself?	__	__
7. When I have seen sagging performance, have I confronted it and positively reinforced the desired behavior?	__	__

If there is a single no answer for any of the above, you have failed. On the other hand, if you have seven honest yeses, the failure lies with the employee.

If the failure is clearly the employee's, you have an obligation to the employee, yourself, and your company to make a career adjustment. Many managers, due to company and other regulations, find it practically impossible to terminate an individual. If this is the case, do everything within your power to have that person transferred to a more suitable job.

If termination must occur, document the causes. With this in mind, keep a record of each time you confront an incompetency.

Many managers shy away from career adjustments. No one enjoys them, but they come with the territory. We have a responsibility to our productive people to maintain an environment conducive to their success. To retain the person who refuses to help himself is unfair to the group.

People usually fail in pairs. Have you ever noticed who your weakest person has lunch with? Almost invariably the answer to that question identifies the next weakest individual. Misery loves company. If more than one person is failing, it gives the failure an excuse. He does not have to be personally accountable if he can take someone down with him. You would fail, too, if you lunched daily with someone who fed you a diet of venom. Terminating employees takes no talent whatsoever. It does take hard work and properly used management skills to do it with a clear conscience.

EVASIVE ACTION PLAN
To Avoid Fatal Error #11 by Refusing to Condone Incompetence

One of the Fortune Group's tools that has proved successful is "The Fortune Action Contract." After every session, most companies have the students complete it as a means of follow-up.

We have provided you with a contract for use with this program.

Instructions for Completing Action Contract

1. Under 1, write down the single most important idea you've heard during this session.
2. Under "How I will use it," write down:
   A. What you're going to do
   B. When you're going to do it
   C. With whom you're going to do it
3. What will be the benefit for you by using this idea?
4. In our sessions, we give the group a sixty-second preparation break, during which each person enters into a contract with the person next to him, someone else in the meeting, the facilitator of the session, or his manager. We suggest that you choose a person to share with.
   A. Tell that person what you're going to do
   B. Tell him how you're going to do it
   C. Tell him how it will benefit you
5. Make sure you write in the date of commitment and follow-up date for the person you have given this contract.

Fortune Action Contract

Because I feel this is the most important idea for me from this chapter, I make a firm commitment to use it within the next seven days.

1. *This is the single most important idea I got out of this chapter* that I can personally apply:

   _____

   _____

   _____

2. This is how I will use it:

_____

_____

_____

3. What I will gain from its use:

_____

_____

_____

4. Someone to share these ideas with:

_____

Date of commitment: _____

Follow-up date: _____

FATAL ERROR

12 Recognize Only Top Performers

If you took all the top performers in your industry and hired them for your company, at the end of a year only one person would hold the number-one spot.

Before you begin to think how fantastically such employees would perform, on the average, I have some bad news for you: You cannot hire all the top performers, and you cannot build any department within a company with only top producers. No matter how great your financial resources, recruiting abilities, or connections, your efforts will fail. Why? Because that many top performers just don't exist, and even if they did, only one person can get the top spot, while the others get the title *also ran.* Yet many managers waste much time trying to make themselves the first person in history to achieve this impossible task. Simultaneously, they unintentionally discourage their middle (or steady) performers, who make up the backbone of any successful organization.

All profitable companies build their business on good, reliable middle producers, plus a few superstars. Whether you deal with sales, public relations, or accounting, if you measure the performance of your people, you will discover the truth of that statement.

All too often we fail to adequately recognize this backbone of our organization that so heavily contributes to our success. Every employee not only deserves, but requires recognition for both individual accomplishments and teamwork efforts, if he is to consistently perform at his optimum level.

In a typical company, however, any recognition the company provides goes to the few elite superstars. One can especially see this in sales organizations. The entire group may perform well above *PAR*, and everyone may make quota. But what happens to the top producer? She is recognized at the annual sales meeting as salesperson of the year, is inducted into the president's club, earns a great income, gets an all-expenses-paid trip for two to an exotic resort, and receives another plaque for the office wall. She deserves every bit of it. And the company gives it to her.

Now what about the middle producers who form the basis for the company's profitability? They all meet their quota, but in most instances, instead of being treated as winners, they are taken for granted. Their managers assume that they know they have won, but never hand out the prize. Therefore such employees feel like part of the herd. The paycheck no longer seems enough. They cry out for personal recognition.

Peters and Waterman describe the importance of such recognition, or lack of it, in *In Search of Excellence:*

> ... We circle all the way to IBM, perhaps one of the biggest and oldest American companies practicing an intense people orientation. The only issue with IBM is how to start describing it. With the seventy-year-old open door policy? The senior Mr. Watson's $1-a-year country club, established for all employees in the 1920s? The philosophy that starts with "respect for the individual"? Lifetime employment? Insistence upon promotion from within? IBM day-care centers, IBM hotels, IBM running tracks and tennis courts? *Monthly* opinion surveys by the personnel department? A very high success rate among salesmen? The intense training? IBM's total history is one of intense people orientation. And as at McDonald's, it's reflected in the tiniest details. Walk into IBM's New York financial branch. The first thing that greets you is a massive floor-to-ceiling bulletin board with glossy photographs of *every* person in the branch hung under the banner: NEW YORK FINANCIAL ... THE DIFFERENCE IS PEOPLE. ...
>
> While IBM explicitly manages to ensure that 70 to 80 percent of its salespeople meet quotas, another company (an IBM competitor in part of its product line) works it so that only 40 percent of the sales force meets its quotas during a typical year. With this approach, at least 60 percent of the salespeople think of themselves as losers. They resent it and

that leads to dysfunctional, unpredictable, frenetic behavior. Label a man a loser and he'll start acting like one.

Creating Winners

We have observed serious recognition problems in many companies, and the problems seem to lie in either of two extremes: recognizing only top producers, as so often happens in organizations such as sales where productivity is easily measured, or failing to recognize at all in those areas not so frequently measured.

When a company pays shirkers at the same rate as the most productive workers, it cuts off incentive, causes self-esteem to wither, and productivity to die. When everyone receives the same cost-of-living increase in pay, it's easy to settle into a lethargic mode; yet company policy, employment contracts, and even other outside forces often dictate the remuneration for a job classification. In many areas, routine mass compensation or using money as a sole means of recognition creates difficulties in stimulating personal improvement and increased output. Why should the secretary who has increased her typing speed to eighty-seven words per minute strive for ninety-five, if the one who continues to type sixty words per minute receives equal recognition? Why should the accountant who discovers a way for the company to reduce its overhead search for additional company savings when persons who exert minimum effort are treated the same? The answer to our challenge is to recognize everyone for accomplishment, and that doesn't mean "big bucks." It requires the personal touch.

The Personal Touch

When it helps people reach their objectives, management functions on its highest level. In order to reach their goals, staff members need to have reasonable yet challenging targets to aim at, and it is the manager's responsibility to organize these, based on the production standards described in Fatal Error #9 and the goals set by each individual employee.

First, break objectives into bite-sized pieces. In most organizations this requires monthly interim goals, which add up to the yearly total. But we need to remember that this does *not* mean twelve equal increments. Almost invariably seasonal influences change the pattern for accomplishment, and the employee's vacation must be considered and built into projections.

Once the annual and monthly objectives are agreed upon, the manager should establish himself as the coach or support system, functioning to help each person reach his goal.

Set individual objectives that change from employee to employee.

Here we really seek progress and personal growth for our people. On a monthly basis, each person should receive recognition for the attainment of his or her objective. That may consist of a three-sentence note of congratulation or a single flower on her desk, a thirty-five-cent candy bar or tomatoes from the manager's garden. The reward may be almost anything (as long as it is consistent with company policies), but needs to be personal, timely, and consistent. Unlike superstar-only recognition systems, here everyone wins.

Superstars, even though they may be egomaniacs when it comes to personal recognition, may not really appreciate it. They've won all their lives. In fact, most only participate in activities at which they know they can excel. Consequently, even though they crave the kudos, they roll off them like water off the back of a duck. On the other hand, the middle producer may not have received personal recognition for years and may find it as addictive as heroin.

When you begin to develop the practice of having your people furnish you with objectives, you will notice several things immediately. Some people hesitate to give management a stated objective. If this is the case, do not push them, since the stated objective must always be in excess of your minimum standard (PAR). If they accomplish this, they have done the job. Leave them alone, and when they see you use the objective as a tool for recognition and team building, they'll come around. Understand that a fearful attitude generates their hesitancy and take steps to determine what caused the problem in communication.

On other occasions people may appear to be totally unrealistic, and their objectives may seem totally unattainable. No matter how skeptical you may be, you should say, "Go get 'em. I'm behind you one hundred percent."

Never tell anyone he can't. Let him prove it to himself. We see this happen in sales organizations all the time. A manager who was considered, while selling, to be an outstanding performer never made over sixty sales per year. A salesperson says, "My objective is to make one hundred." The manager immediately defeats that person when he says, "Come down to earth. You'll never make it." We should never superimpose our limitations upon others. They may very well do what they say.

If time proves that they were overenthusiastic, guide them in setting a more realistic, yet challenging objective. In such a situation the quality of management becomes most visible. The manager faces quite a challenge when he has to keep someone feeling like a winner when he's staring disappointment in the eye.

Some seize the opportunity to show their power by humiliating the salesperson and not releasing him from the objective. "What's the matter with you? You told me you would accomplish this, but I see you just don't live up to your promises, do you?"

Taking this stance destroys the employee, and everyone loses. Instead, show him how much progress he made and encourage him to keep moving toward a more practical challenge. Again, let him set the challenge. He should not be told to work toward a low target because that's the best he can possibly do. Instead let him feel the dignity and confidence that go with setting his own objective.

If you report objectives for your department to upper-level management, you do no one a favor by reporting wildly unrealistic objectives. Never set your objectives on what the employees say they can do. In fact, I suggest to corporate management that they not base corporate objectives on what managers say they can do. Managers on all levels need to be conservative, while allowing for the possibility of a miracle. Miracles do happen, but you cannot count on them as regular occurrences.

Team Building

I would also like to suggest that you take a long, hard look at any contest that you use in an attempt to stimulate productivity. Our experience has shown that most become a waste of money, counterproductive, or a combination of the two. While many managers swear *by* them, I'll guarantee that their people swear *at* them. What on the surface may appear as fun and games may not be fun to others at all. When I use the term *contest* I do not include the standard forms of recognition that you use to honor your superstars for exceptional performance. I refer instead to competitions that pit your people against one another. The vast majority of people have a naturally competitive spirit, without management turning it into a street fight.

Over the years I've always thought the most insidious contest was the steak-and-beans dinner used by many sales organizations. The traditional approach divides the organization into two teams and has them compete with each other for a set period of time. They top off the contest with a dinner where the winners are served steak in the presence of the losers, who eat beans. I recently heard of a twist that was such a bad idea that it seemed almost ridiculous. This group invited the spouses and dates of both winners and losers, and you guessed it, the losers' guests also received the humiliating plate of beans.

If any organization tracks the effects of a contest, they can note that certainly during the contest, production increases. Immediately thereafter a fall-off occurs, and in practically every case, sales drop below normal levels, and they lose people. It would have been far better never to have engaged in the endeavor.

Where we do not recommend contests, we do recommend games. There's a lot of difference between the two. A contest aims at increased productivity, and it's always structured so that you have a few winners and a lot of losers. The game makes it fun to work with your company, and you might be surprised to see how productive people become when they really enjoy their jobs. Furthermore, in the sales game everyone wins. It takes the form of a team objective, which can be the completion of a project, maintenance of a safety record, sales objective, or any other endeavor where you measure performance. When the objective is reached, all members of the team receive an equal reward.

A friend of mine who operates a sales organization conducts my favorite game. Each month the salespeople in his office set a challenging objective based on the volume generated in that month for the previous year. It is never less than a 20 percent increase. In those months where they reach the objective, every person in the office (including salespeople, the secretaries, bookkeeper, and even the shipping clerk) receive an award, and they are all of equal monetary value. Compare this with the usual practice of recognizing the two or three outstanding sales performers, ignoring the other salespeople, and never even taking into consideration that much of the sales success directly results from the efforts of the support staff. My friend never announces awards in advance, and uses a lot of showmanship to make it exciting. I was present on February 4th, 1984, when at three o'clock in the afternoon Santa Claus appeared, red suit and all, with a big pack on his back, containing a Christmas gift for each member of the staff, in recognition of their January production. The gifts ranged from perfume to clock radios. I must admit my favorites were the Cabbage Patch dolls. This organization has its share of personality conflicts, yet they function as a team because everyone gets appreciated for his efforts, and it's fun to work there.

Above All: Respect

People *will* scramble for recognition, and many do feel starved for it, but each worker also needs something much more basic from management. What is this simple truth that managers should recognize, but often pass by? That everyone needs respect from management.

For example one investment firm refers to one-half of its staff as "the professionals" and the rest of the employees as "office staff." While the "office staff" members, primarily secretaries, do not expect to earn the wages of the Ivy League grads with multiple degrees, they resent the inference that if one group is "professional," it follows that everyone else is "unprofessional."

Moreover, the secretaries know very well that many clients have greater direct contact with the "office staff" than with "the professionals," and a large measure of the customers' level of satisfaction remains in the hands of the support staff. Management knows that, too, but doesn't acknowledge the fact. When performance-recognition times occur, the company celebrates "the professionals'" accomplishments in

Chart 14
Recognition Review

How can I create more opportunities for recognition?

How can my staff acquire recognition now?

a variety of ways: bonuses, company cars, trips, and award dinners. On the other hand, they remember the "office staff" with uniform cost-of-living raises and a flower on National Secretaries' Day. Management was incredulous last year when one secretary started a chain reaction by placing her rose in the trash can. I contend that the same woman would have been thrilled if the rose had arrived in response to some work accomplishment.

A different firm in the same field considers its counselors and support staff directly associated. One or more counselors and a secretary form a team, and the company directly ties the secretary's bonuses or other forms of recognition to the performance of the people she supports. Here, esprit de corps runs at stratospheric levels, yet annual take-home pay on the secretarial level does not quite equal that paid the office staff in the first company.

Recognition and respect, the foods of the spirit! Every well-managed business affords its employees the opportunity of earning all they need.

What opportunities exist for your people to acquire recognition? What new opportunities can you create? List them in Chart 14. Put them into action and watch productivity accelerate.

It's simple to avoid Fatal Error #12. All you have to do is give credit *when* it's due. Like today. And give it to every employee whenever he or she stretches or meets new objectives.

EVASIVE ACTION PLAN
To Avoid Fatal Error #12 by Creating Winners

One of the Fortune Group's tools that has proved successful is "The Fortune Action Contract." After every session, most companies have the students complete it as a means of follow-up.

We have provided you with a contract for use with this program.

Instructions for Completing Action Contract

1. Under 1, write down the single most important idea you've heard during this session.
2. Under "How I will use it," write down:
   A. What you're going to do
   B. When you're going to do it
   C. With whom you're going to do it
3. What will be the benefit for you by using this idea?
4. In our sessions, we give the group a sixty-second preparation break, during which each person enters into a contract with the person next to him, someone else in the

meeting, the facilitator of the session, or his manager. We
suggest that you choose a person to share with.
    A. Tell that person what you're going to do
    B. Tell him how you're going to do it
    C. Tell him how it will benefit you
  5. Make sure you write in the date of commitment and fol-
     low-up date for the person you have given this contract.

Fortune Action Contract

Because I feel this is the most important idea for me from this chapter, I make a firm commitment to use it within the next seven days.

  1. *This is the single most important idea I got out of this
     chapter* that I can personally apply:

     _____

     _____

     _____

  2. This is how I will use it:

     _____

     _____

     _____

  3. What I will gain from its use:

     _____

     _____

     _____

  4. Someone to share these ideas with:

     _____

Date of commitment: _____

Follow-up date: _____

FATAL ERROR 13

Try to Manipulate People

The previous chapters have examined a series of concepts that go into the building of a foundation for successful management, against a backdrop of common management errors. Before addressing the last issue, let me review a few of these foundation concepts.

1. Management is the skill of obtaining predetermined objectives through and with the voluntary cooperation of others
2. The purpose of management is to provide for the continuation of the business, even in our absence
3. The generation of a profit is mandatory in order for the business to continue, for customers to be served, and for obligations to employees to be met
4. People succeed or fail based on their habits
5. People do not try unless two questions can be answered positively: What are my chances of success? and where is the value—measured in self-esteem—to me?
6. A manager's job is to induce people to behave properly
7. In order to influence the behavior of people, we cannot deal with just behavior; we must deal with people's thinking patterns
8. Management is a thinking—not a doing—job

Changing Attitudes

In each of these concepts I have stressed that a person's performance directly relates to the way he thinks (or his *attitude*). As managers we can change the attitudes of our people, but we must also take care in the methods we use to influence those on our staff. Good influences will add to the self-esteem of those on our staff and will make them more productive. Bad ones will cause the staff to feel manipulated, and production will be negatively affected.

Take Attitude Into Account

If you doubt the importance of attitude, consider this. Suppose a knock at the door now interrupted your reading, and you answered it to discover you had just inherited $5 million from a distant relative. Your thinking about many things, from the value of continuing to read to the value of continuing to work would change, wouldn't it? You might find yourself with many new friends, or all your family might suddenly turn against you. Attitude change comes with altered circumstances.

ENVIRONMENT CHANGE. In much the same way, vary any human's environment, and an attitude change follows. As a major element in your employees' environment, every action you take has an impact on their attitudes. Repaint an office, change the pay scale, rework your line, alter a work pattern: Weigh every such action's possible effect beforehand, because the influence on your employees' thinking could be positive or negative.

The troublesome part of this attempt to change attitudes is that these changes do not last. The new paint job fades, and so does its effect on office morale. The new product that raised spirits may not continue to do so when the competition introduces a superior one. The welcomed wage increase soon becomes taken for granted as inflation further erodes it. On the other hand, the initial changes in environment could have had a negative effect. If you ordered the paint job for some offices but not all, the slighted employees may feel you played favorites. If the new product seems to some to lack appeal or the wage change takes the form of a cut, negative attitudes ensue. Nonetheless, over time even negative attitudes will fade to some degree.

KNOWLEDGE AND EDUCATION. Another way to change thinking is to use knowledge, ideas, education, and training. These have a far more lasting effect than the changes in condition or environment, because an idea that has taken root has a tendency to survive. Each person's fundamental beliefs always surface, to have a final say over his actions.

We at the Fortune Group have polled both managers and sales-people in practically every business for their opinion concerning what increases the salespeople's performance. Opinions always differ. Managers cite better work habits; salespeople normally say more prospects. Both are right, yet neither is entirely correct. The salesman really needs greater confidence, which will result in better work habits and a high closing ratio. Both could result from training the salesperson to close more effectively, because once he has developed that skill, it will stay with him for years. The money management pours into a change in conditions, a new direct-mail program, or any other indirect alteration will not alter his closing ratio at all. Or if it does change anything, it will be temporary. For long-term change, invest in education and training to help your staff.

CLOSE YOUR "ATTITUDE SALES."　When we strip away the ornamentation of management, underneath we find that in many ways every manager acts as a salesperson whose prospects are the people he manages. If he suddenly announces a new workload, some change in office atmosphere, or a new pay scale, he will need to sell it to those he manages, and his closing ratio clearly measures his command of the skills of management. Effective leadership requires that your people cooperate voluntarily, not as a result of manipulative action on your part.

Know Your People

If there exists a secret to managing effectively and without manipulation, it is *know your people*. I mean, really *know* them. We stated that management is a thinking—not doing—job, and management should think about its people.

Years ago, many of us in management took the attitude that if a person's problem did not directly relate to the job, it didn't concern us. We mistakenly tried to divide our people's lives into neat areas or boxes. Often we assumed several people made up the employee: the working person, the family person, the social, cultural, and spiritual person. The harder managers tried to make this concept work, the sooner we saw it did not. Man is an integrated whole, and we cannot divide him into tidy little compartments. We must deal with the whole person. If an individual has a problem at home, it will influence him at work. Employment problems also affect family lives. Social and financial problems impact upon job performance.

We need to know our people individually mainly because any given condition will affect different people in different ways. When some people have a problem at home, they cannot function at work. Others cannot function at work unless they have a problem at home.

Effective management often requires understanding the pressures impacting upon our people, so they can receive the support they need. Yet a manager faces the danger of becoming personally involved. If you become a marriage counselor or financial advisor, you overstep your boundaries. Despite the pitfalls, you must thoroughly understand each of your people in order to manage them so that they will not feel taken advantage of.

Kent Stickler, noted consultant to the financial industry, relates the following example of outside pressures affecting employee performance.

An experienced teller with several years of excellent service with a major financial institution worked the drive-in window. A time-pressured customer felt that her service was slow and told her as much. She snapped back using profanity.

Of course the customer complained. The young woman's manager felt shocked at this inconsistent behavior. The manager confronted the teller and discovered that two months earlier the woman's husband had deserted her and their three children. Prior to leaving, he had made numerous charges to their credit cards and had taken all their savings. Recognizing the importance of her credit reputation to her employment with the bank, she had taken a part-time job. She was working as a waitress until 2:00 A.M. During this entire period she had been operating on no more than four hours sleep a night and had spent a good portion of her waking hours worrying about her children, who stayed at home alone.

Fortunately, the manager recognized the value of a proven employee and knew that outside pressures affect performance. The manager immediately arranged for a loan from the bank, with payments the employee could handle. This removed the pressure of the debts incurred by the husband. Her manager insisted the teller take a day of vacation to get some rest. Two days later she came back to her job and functioned effectively.

Knowing your people is absolutely essential if my previous statement that every manager acts as a salesperson whose prospects are the people he manages has any validity. Selling is nothing more than communicating. Communication does not begin with being understood, but with understanding others.

Making Management Work

Throughout my career with the Fortune Group I have spent the majority of my time conducting management seminars. Without fail we have emphasized in each that a manager holds the major responsibility of influencing the thinking of people. I've told many groups that, even though they may not like the comparison, management is analogous to preaching. It is your business whether or not you go to church but if you do, you will see the same person present the same message to essentially the same people week after week. We know this because attendance at our churches doesn't vary by 5 percent from week to week. Do you know why the minister or priest continues this effort? He recognizes that if he can elevate the level of thinking of his congregation by one iota, he has done his job.

Without exception, I found managers like to hear their job requires that they elevate the thinking of their people. This excites them and gives them a sense of self-esteem. Unfortunately it also makes the job seem overly conceptual.

A manager's job, however, is not conceptual, but pragmatic. Every day he or she must deal with realities of life, which take the form of various pressures. Monthly overhead, payrolls, production, sales quotas are tangible and must be dealt with immediately. These stresses often defeat us, and we seek to get quick results without looking at the long-term effects our actions will have. While you must reach daily objectives, don't expect immediate solutions for long-range problems. There is no quick fix.

Approaches to Increased Productivity

Because of such pressures we all tend to favor approaches to increasing productivity that seem expedient in the short run yet create greater problems for the future. But these nonproductive methods usually create bad feelings, and cause our employees to feel as if they are treated unfairly. Trying to *work* our way out of this vicious circle will not be effective, but we can *think* our way out of it. Unfortunately we have not always thought—at least not about our people.

In all of industrial history we have developed only three approaches for getting employees to produce more. Every motivational scheme falls into one of these three broad categories:

> Fear
> Rewards
> Belief building

For the most part the two most often used have proven largely counterproductive, because they generate short spurts of activity and do nothing to build the group.

FEAR. Historically, this has been the most common motivational approach. And it smacks of manipulation. The manager normally uses it in one of two ways—either threat or actual punishment. First, let's look at threat.

> "Produce or lose your job."
> "Produce or be humiliated in front of your peers."
> "Produce or suffer any other dire consequences."

More often than not, the threat takes the form of a loss of personal dignity or esteem within the organization. True, if an individual (or a group) wishes to keep the job or please you badly enough, you can frighten him into performing. But over the long haul (and that's a matter of just a few weeks), the use of threat or fear as a motivational tool results in withdrawal or hostility on the part of the one threatened.

Not many managers will admit to using a threat or fear as a motivational tool, but it occurs frequently and is usually done unconsciously. A manager has sixteen people under his supervision. Thirteen perform at *PAR* or better; they are genuinely exciting employees. The other three do not respond. The manager gives it everything he has, but it only results in his own anger and frustration. Before he realizes it, he stands in front of the group at a staff meeting, saying, "Did you hear that? Did you hear the bell ring? I don't know whether or not you heard it, but the bell rang, and that means school is out, children! From now on, there are going to be some changes around here; in this department, you grow—or go!"

The manager or supervisor did not really talk to his entire group. He attempted to reach the three who were not responding. But those three derelict employees didn't hear a word he said. It went right over their heads. The thirteen productive individuals do hear, and they leave the meeting alienated.

Even Harold Geneen, who was an awe-inspiring CEO, realized that fear proved counterproductive:

> To the degree that business commanders strike fear in the hearts of their management teams, they have turned the American business world into a jungle, where scared people compete *within* a company for their own personal survival. In the long run, I am certain it is counterproductive. First of all, frightened people play office politics; they won't admit their problems early enough for them to be solved. The most capable, independent people leave, not willing to work under those conditions. Good people don't want to come into such a company. Imperceptibly at first, and then more and more, all these negative conditions and attitudes will feed upon one another until, in the end, the company will slide into a decline that the chief executive and his board of directors will find difficult to fathom.

No matter what the pressures, resist the temptation to call the troops together and threaten them. Never call your group on the carpet through the use of a "hot" letter or memo. On the other hand, do not hesitate, as we recommended in Fatal Error #11, to get with an individual, one-on-one, and confront in private, using the prescribed technique. When you confront face-to-face and look a one-person audience in the eye, you'll tend to hold your anger in check and think before speaking. And as you use this method you will not alienate your entire staff while achieving nothing with the person whose behavior you wished to change.

The second aspect of fear as a motivational tool involves the use of actual punishment. As with threats, punishment does nothing to re-direct the employee to desired behavior. Many managers punish be-cause that action rewards or reinforces the punisher. Even though it destroys the relationship with the employee and damages the organiza-tion, if severe enough, punishment will stop undesired behavior, and the manager gets what he wants immediately. If he punishes frequently he soon gains the reputation among the employees as a person who's constantly attempting to catch people doing something wrong. The manager then becomes a precedent to punishment and employees avoid him. Avoidance or withdrawal is one of the least dangerous of employee reactions to punishment. Hostility in the form of sabotage, vandalism, theft, and work slowdowns are just as likely to occur. Practi-cally every business has experienced some form of this reaction.

A number of years ago, I went to dinner at one of the most fashion-able restaurants in Milwaukee. Shortly after ordering, my waiter in-formed me that they could not serve me. They had to close for the evening. When I inquired why, he told me that a disgruntled employee had exchanged salt and sugar in the kitchen. The chef triggered the in-cident by dressing down a busboy in front of the entire staff. The ex-change of condiments was the employee's act of retaliation before quitting.

In some instances, managers punish without fully understanding what they're doing, especially in sales organizations. Many make it a practice to rank their salespeople in order of productivity and display it. Others mail such rankings to the salespersons' homes, where their families can see them. Discussing this practice with many managers has shown me most feel they use this as a method of recognizing their top performers. Those who head the list may receive some satisfaction, but once you pass the top two or three, it becomes punishment, partic-ularly to those in the lower 50 percent.

If you try to use punishment, you may find the results unpredictable, because what you consider punishment may not appear that way to others at all. To the shirking employee, a day off without pay may seem another day's vacation. I know of a firm employing door-to-door sales-people, which elected to punish its lowest producer at each monthly sales meeting. The punishment consisted of the manager throwing a pie into the face of the nonperformer. I'm not sure what effect they ex-pected, but it immediately became a game. The nonperformer received an enormous amount of attention and became the life of the party.

Management continues to ignore the fact that the recipient of the pie always laughs and that their nonperformers even compete for this position.

Severe punishment is invariably more effective than mild. But the severity of punishment great enough to have any real effect would be against the law.

REWARDS.   Our second management motivational approach takes the exact opposite tack of fear and involves rewards and incentives. These, too, definitely work—temporarily. Yes, if you stimulate people enough or excite them by the offer of some type of "carrot," they will perform. Yet the things people regard as an incentive today very quickly become their right—then they no longer stimulate. So, to recreate the excitement, you've got to offer yet another incentive. Eventually you have nothing left to give.

Recognition should be of the team-building variety. We warn you to look at all incentives beyond this with a jaundiced eye. Many of the things we in management regard as motivators (such as pension plans, profit-sharing programs, insurance, and other employee benefits) are not motivators at all. They may aid in recruiting and, to some extent, in retaining people, but since we can not directly tie them into measurable performance, their motivational effect is neutral.

In some instances, incentives even serve as punishers. I recently attended a new product kickoff meeting in a multinational organization. The sales manager announced that each employee who sold the required amount in a ninety-day time period would receive a $150 gift certificate. He then laughingly informed the group that their spouses would be informed of this opportunity, and the gift certificate would be in the spouse's name. The single members of the organization laughed uproariously. Some of the married people forced a smile. Others muttered to themselves. For any person in the group experiencing marital difficulty, the $150 incentive acted as a punisher.

BELIEF BUILDERS.   The third motivational approach is that of belief building. This philosophy differs dramatically from the manipulative characteristics inherent in the use of fear and rewards.

Essentially every management effort falls into one of two categories: manipulating or building. The manipulators far outnumber the builders, as it's human nature to manipulate. Manipulation, using fear and incentive, produces an immediate result, coupled with long-range problems. The only way I know to avoid manipulation is to identify the thinking that precedes it. Managers', like salespeople's, actions directly result from thought patterns. When we feel that our team fails to produce in the manner it should, we will invariably ask ourselves why. If we think, *They don't want to. If they really wanted to produce, they would,* we have stepped on the road to manipulation. Next we ask our-

Chart 15
Belief-Building Review

How have I tried to change people's thinking using the techniques below?	How have they worked?	What can I do to improve each situation?
Fear:		
Rewards:		
Belief building:		
Fear:		
Rewards:		
Belief building:		
Fear:		
Rewards:		
Belief building:		

selves, *How can I make them want to produce?* We answer, *I'll give them a special reward that will make them want to.* Some may try the more counterproductive approach of, *I'll get them together and let them know I'm going to hurt them if they don't respond. That will make them want to produce.* Either of these approaches acts out manipulation. The manager has done nothing to direct the employee into the profitable activity or deal with the problems causing the lack of production. He has simply arranged a set of circumstances designed to bribe or force his people to perform.

In contrast a belief builder recognizes that if people do not perform at a *PAR* level, it is not because they do not want to succeed (unless, of course, they have withdrawn or are rebelling against management's previous attempts to manipulate them). He knows that lack of belief generates the lack of performance. Truly productive people achieve much because of their inner strengths. Productivity therefore reflects the individual's belief in himself, his company, and the products and services they render. Overuse of fear and rewards destroys these essential characteristics. When people are manipulated, especially with threats, they feel as if they have prostituted themselves. Subsequently they lose self-esteem and come to resent the organization and the individual who put them in this demeaning situation. Review the methods you have used, on Chart 15, and make plans for improvements.

Any time you work out an idea that you feel will help you stay within that budget, meet that quota, reach that goal, ask yourself these questions:

1. Will that idea build pride in my people?
2. Will it build belief in our products and services?
3. Will it build belief in the company?

These are questions that leaders ask themselves. They will also attempt to deal with others in the fashion outlined in Chart 16, by building others, rather than manipulating them.

If the idea detracts in any way from this value system, it is a poor one. Don't use it! Search for one that builds pride in these three areas.

A Creed for Leaders

Why have many successful businesses written credos or mission statements? Why would these documents be worth the time spent developing them?

If you study business credos, you will soon see that all express positive thoughts about the buying public and contribute to the self-images of those within the organization. Because the people who have such

Chart 16
Builders Versus Manipulators

BUILDER	MANIPULATOR
Sincere concern for other people	Tunnel vision
Supportive	Self-oriented
Good with other people's objectives	Power hungry
Developer	Deals in threat/fear
Consistent	Oppressive
Disciplined	User of people
Equitable	Uses power for own gain
Confronts deviations	Concentrates on problems, not objectives
Enthusiastic	Closed minded
Patient	Resists change
Good personal self-image	Externalist
Good finding	"Me first" attitude
Perceptive	Inconsistent
Praises success	Impatient
Feels competition is healthy	Short-term
Feels change is an opportunity and	Insecure
a fact of life	Refuses to delegate
Intuitive	Selfish
	Jealous
	Feels threatened

belief systems in their companies automatically develop pride in their company and perform better, all successful companies hold tightly to such philosophies.

Whatever their size today, all companies at one time were small businesses. I understand the total sales volume for Coca-Cola was $55.00 its first year of business. Every small business at some point stood on the brink of disaster. The strength that got it through the trying times did not rely on the desire for money alone, because there was no money; that power came from an individual. Every company owes its success to being fortunate enough to have had the man or woman who could face the challenges of the moment. Strength of character produces enough resiliency to fight back. Under the most severe pressures, people win because they manage and perform in accordance with the Law of Compensation. This law, simply stated, is "compensation is in direct proportion to the quality and quantity of service rendered." I would strongly recommend that all managers focus the thinking of their people on a corporate philosophy or credo, preferably written, that encompasses the Law of Compensation.

I have elected, somewhat hesitantly, at the urging of the people I manage, to include the corporate philosophy of the Fortune Group. Our business is founded on a verse of Scripture. It may seem an unlikely precept for management, but in the early days, when times were tough and it seemed that everything conspired against our business success, I found this particular Bible verse, John 10:10, kept me going:

> The thief cometh not, but for to steal, and to kill, and to destroy: I am come that they might have life, and that they might have it more abundantly.

It seemed to me that the thief took many forms: disappointment, disillusionment, discouragement, and lack of pride. I reasoned that we at the Fortune Group, through our training systems, warred with those things that steal promise and profit and kill a living enterprise. Recognizing that we might have employees who might not relate to the Bible, this was translated into the credo of "helping people help themselves": helping managers avoid errors and build leadership qualities, helping employees acquire the skills to perform successfully, helping individuals develop the disciplines necessary for success. I believe the greatest management challenge for each of us begins in making sure that on a daily basis our credos become our personal objective and that, by example, in effective management we influence our employees to feel the same way.

Corporate Philosophy

A business is an entity existing primarily in the financial world; however, the Fortune Group believes that businesses must exist for some higher purpose than their financial aspects alone. A business is not a master to be served by people, but should itself serve. The reason for our existence is to serve the higher purpose of *"helping people help themselves."*

We believe in regard to:

Services and Products—that they should be of superior quality—the very best that we can provide. We refuse to offer a product or service in which we do not believe and cannot take personal pride. We will always offer maximum value for every dollar invested.

Customers and Clients—they are the foundation of our business. Our only true asset is our ability to serve them. In all of our dealings we will be honest, truthful, and strive to serve their best interest.

Employees and Associates—We respect the value of those associated with us as fellow humans and their right of self-determination in setting their own career objectives. We will never regard people as objects or pawns to be used for the purpose of management. To the best of our ability we will afford those associated with us as a career opportunity where their personal objectives may be reached. The environment within our group shall be such that those who are so motivated can develop personally, seek advancement, and earn greater success without forfeiting their right to fail.

Competitors—We do not compete with those who serve. We endorse their efforts and seek only to cooperate. Our only competition, if any, comes from those who mislead, misguide, or take unfair advantage.

Profit—We believe in making a fair and honest profit. The continuation of our business and its ability to fulfill its purpose is dependent upon profit. We refuse to deal with any of our publics on an unprofitable basis, lest we fail them all.

EVASIVE ACTION PLAN
To Avoid Fatal Error #13 by Building Belief

One of the Fortune Group's tools that has proved successful is "The Fortune Action Contract." After every session, most companies have the students complete it as a means of follow-up.

We have provided you with a contract for use with this program.

Instructions for Completing Action Contract

1. Under 1, write down the single most important idea you've heard during this session.
2. Under "How I will use it," write down:
   A. What you're going to do
   B. When you're going to do it
   C. With whom you're going to do it
3. What will be the benefit for you by using this idea?
4. In our sessions, we give the group a sixty-second preparation break, during which each person enters into a contract with the person next to him, someone else in the meeting, the facilitator of the session, or his manager. We suggest that you choose a person to share with.
   A. Tell that person what you're going to do
   B. Tell him how you're going to do it
   C. Tell him how it will benefit you
5. Make sure you write in the date of commitment and follow-up date for the person you have given this contract.

Fortune Action Contract

Because I feel this is the most important idea for me from this chapter, I make a firm commitment to use it within the next seven days.

1. *This is the single most important idea I got out of this chapter* that I can personally apply:

   _____

   _____

   _____

2. This is how I will use it:

   _____

   _____

   _____

3. What I will gain from its use:

    _____

    _____

    _____

4. Someone to share these ideas with:

    _____

Date of commitment: _____

Follow-up date: _____